The church world-wide is experi_____ ...... naturally causes the subject of apostleship to assume increasing importance. Bill Scheidler has certainly given us a "fresh look" at the meaning of an apostle for our time. His presentation is truly significant, greatly important—and one of the best available. Thoroughly scriptural and practical, the explanation of apostolic function, preparation, mentoring, and authority is excellent, bringing much needed balance and biblical reference to today's discussion. His book would be my first recommendation on the subject.

—ERNEST GENTILE

Author of *Worship God!*, *Your Sons and Daughters Shall Prophesy,* and *The Final Triumph*

A reasonably familiar saying runs like this: "The only thing we learn from history is that we never learn from history." Church history shows how often the pendulum of truth seems to swing from one extreme to the other. This is certainly so when it comes to the ministry of apostles. For the Cessationist school of thought, apostles ceased to exist at the death of the apostle John, the beloved. For the Restorationist school of thought, apostles are to be found anywhere and everywhere, having degrees of power and authority in the church and over the church. Descriptions, authority, power, and function of apostles are many and varied.

Bill Scheidler's book comes as a 'relief' from, on the one hand, rejection and unbelief of apostleship, and on the other hand, over-exultation and almost deification of the apostolic ministry. Bill presents true apostolic ministry as servanthood and fatherhood!

i

Having known Bill personally for many years, and his character qualities, I have no hesitation in recommending his text to the greater body of Christ, as a balancing view on this necessary ministry in the church in these final days. For those who read the book—'Simple, clear and easy to read'—enjoy "Apostles: The Fathering Servant."

—KEVIN J. CONNER

Author of *The Church in the New Testament, The Foundations of Christian Doctrine,* and *Interpreting the Symbols and Types*

APOSTLES

THE FATHERING SERVANT

A Fresh
Biblical
Perspective
on Their
Role Today

BILL SCHEIDLER
WITH DICK IVERSON

CITYBIBLE
PUBLISHING

Portland, Oregon, U.S.A.

PUBLISHED BY CITY BIBLE PUBLISHING
9200 NE FREMONT, PORTLAND, OREGON 97220
Printed in U.S.A.

City Bible Publishing is a ministry of City Bible Church and is dedicated to serving the local church and its leaders through the production and distribution of quality restoration materials.

It is our prayer that these materials, proven in the context of the local church, will equip leaders in exalting the Lord and extending His kingdom.

For a free catalog of additional resources from City Bible Publishing please call 1-800-777-6057 or visit our website at www.citybiblepublishing.com.

Apostles: The Fathering Servant
© Copyright 2001 by Bill Scheidler

International Standard Book Number: 1-886849-81-1

Library of Congress Cataloging-in-Publication Data

Scheidler, Bill, 1947-
    Apostles, the fathering servant : a fresh biblical perspective on their role today / Bill Scheidler with Dick Iverson.
        p. cm.
    ISBN 1-886849-81-1 (pbk. : alk. paper)
    1. Apostolate (Christian theology)--Biblical teaching.   I.
Iverson, Dick. II. Title.
    BS2545.A67 S34 2002
    262'.1--dc21

                            2001006840

Dedication

I would like to dedicate this book to three men who have been fathers to me who have made a tremendous impact on my life. The first two are true apostolic fathers who have given me insight and understanding concerning God's purposes for the Church, Dick Iverson and Kevin Conner. The other man is my own natural father, Ralph Scheidler, who laid a strong foundation in my life through his excellent example in matters of honesty, integrity, loyalty, and faithfulness.

Table of Contents

Introduction

Foreword

This book, Apostles: The Fathering Servant, *is biblical, systematic, thorough, fair, insightful, and viable. I recommend all to read, study, and apply the principles from this book. We need many more true spiritual fathers who have the spiritual capacity to nurture leaders and churches: servants with a father's heart. Well done, Bill! This book is a great contribution to the Body of Christ.*

The interest concerning the subject of apostles has grown immense-ly in the last several years. I personally welcome a new appreciation of this valuable ministry and a new understanding. I have known Bill for 25 years, we have traveled together nationally and internationally, we were on the Portland Bible College teaching staff together, and, most recently, work together ministering to our fellowship of ministers called Ministers Fellowship International. Bill is a man of integrity, a man of principle and a balanced teacher of the Word of God.

— **FRANK DAMAZIO**
Senior Pastor, City Bible Church
November 2001

Apostolic Confusion

Just what is an apostle? I was listening to the radio the other day in my car when the talk show host referred to himself as the "apostle of truth." I thought it was an intriguing personal application of a biblical word that has no tangible parallel in the real world. It made me think about how other people might define the word.

If you look up the word "apostle" in a dictionary, it does not define the word in contemporary terms, but points you back to the New Testament Age and the biblical record. Or it may make some reference to the church world, particularly the Mormon Church, where the term has been used most frequently in the last century. Defining the term "apostle" is therefore more difficult than simply looking it up in the dictionary.

One of the problems with defining the term is that it is foreign to most of our cultures. If you use the term "teacher," everyone knows immediately what you are talking about and it is very easy to define. It is the same with the terms, "doctor" or "pilot." The terms are easily defined and point us to a specific function. But how do we define the term "apostle" and then understand what function an apostle is to have?

Because there is no contemporary, cultural point of reference for this term, it leaves the whole concept of apostolic function a matter of personal interpretation. Defining the function can then be based on personal experience, past instruction on the subject, or personal study. The result is a wide range of views on an increasingly important subject in the church today.

Apostolic ministry, along with all other ministries of the body of Christ, cannot be open to any and all definitions. If that were allowed, it would be simple to compose a definition that authenticates a preconceived function rather than making our function conform to the biblical model. In defining ministry function, we must define it from a biblical basis.

The term "apostle" is foreign to our vocabulary. That causes confusion about how the function of an apostle should be defined. In the church world today, there is much confusion about how to define the function of an apostle. One could literally talk to fifteen different people and get fifteen different definitions apostolic function. Some might define an apostle in the past tense, as if it was a function or ministry that belongs to the historical record of the early church. This view suggests that apostles existed for a short period of time under the direct administration of Jesus and their function was limited to laying the doctrinal foundations for the primitive church. This view also suggests that this ministry no longer functions in the church today.

Some might speak of apostles in the future tense, indicating that the word "apostle" refers to a handful of ministries that will arrive on the scene prior to the second coming of Christ. They would argue that some of these future apostles will be true and some will be numbered among the false ministries that are predicted to be prevalent in the last days.

Others might disagree with these positions and argue that apostles do indeed exist in the world today. They would say it is a ministry function that was given to the church by Christ when He ascended into heaven and is to be fully functioning in the church until His return.

To go even deeper, if you ask this last group of people to discuss the concept of apostolic function further, you will get a wide variety of answers. In some cases, the definition will be so generic that, when all is said and done, everyone can be defined as an apostle. In other cases, the definition is so exalted that no one could ever hope to attain to it, and if they did, they would undoubtedly be overtaken with pride and disqualify themselves immediately from the ministry.

Just for fun, I asked a group of pastors and church leaders to write down their definition of an apostle. I received some interesting answers. Here is a sample of what I received:

"An apostle is a seasoned ministry who has pastored at least seven years."

"An apostle is one who sets things in order."

"An apostle is a messenger of vision, an equipper and overseer of pastors."

"An apostle has broad influence, he oversees and helps extend the work of the body of Christ."

"An apostle is one with a heart and gift to reach the lost."

"An apostle is one who supervises a pastoral team."

"An apostle is a revealer of the mysteries of God, a man of much revelation knowledge and a unique authority from God."

"An apostle is one endued with divine power and a divine message."

"An apostle supports the other ministries by providing covering."

"An apostle has churches he is recognized and received by."

"An apostle is an ambassador, a delegate, commissioned by someone to represent him."

"An apostle brings discipline to the churches."

"Apostolic ministry is carried on by leaders who take the gospel where it has not gone before."

"An apostle is one sent from God to establish and build. His spiritual authority is indicated by the miraculous signs and wonders by which God confirms his ministry. His main function is raising godly leadership."

These responses come from pastors and church leaders – I wonder how diverse the comments would be if you asked members of the congregations in those same churches. Needless to say, there are a lot of people who have a variety of ideas regarding what the function of an apostle really is.

I had an interesting conversation recently with a pastor from Greece. He was talking about how English speakers tend to do a lot of damage to the Greek language when they preach (at which point I determined never to make references to what the Greek says when I am preaching in Greece). He went on to say, "I don't know what the big deal is nowadays about the function of apostles. In Greece an apostle is simply a messenger. It is not uncommon to see an ad in the paper, 'Wanted: Apostle. Must have his own bicycle.'" That reality could certainly adjust some of our concepts.

Unless we can sift through all of the cultural trends, historical misconceptions, personal biases, and doctrinal limitations, we run the risk of being deprived of a truly awesome ministry that was given as a gift by Christ to the church that will help equip the church and bring it to maturity. Our definition of apostolic function cannot come from those sources. Instead, we must define apostolic function from a source that is undisputed and unchanging. Our definition must be based on a truth, not opinion.

To do this, we must start with the Bible as the clearly revealed word of God. God must be the source of how we define apostolic function. Our definition must be based on what the Bible teaches, not on what we would personally like to believe. We must base our definition on God's ideal, not on our traditional concepts that generally tend to limit God's ability to work through us.

As we do this, I think we will find that biblical, apostolic ministry is a fathering ministry given to the church to assist people, leaders, and individual local churches in coming to a place of maturity. We will find that apostolic ministry is also a serving ministry that stands along side of other ministries to lift and encourage them in the fulfillment of their respective destinies. In other words, an apostle is to be a fathering servant.

This is not necessarily the image being presented today through much of what is said concerning this ministry. It is only Christ's ministry of the apostle as presented and defined in the Bible that we desire to see brought forth in this day. We are not as interested in personal experience or opinions. We want to see apostolic ministry as it is truly represented in the Word of God.

As we explore this ministry together, I pray that we can tap into the unsearchable riches of Christ and that the Holy Spirit will lead us and guide us into all truth.

MINISTRY MOTIVATION

"Whoever desires to become great among you shall be your servant. And whoever of you desires to be first shall be slave of all. For even the Son of Man did not come to be served, but to serve, and to give His life a ransom for many."

(MARK 10:43B-45)

Whenever you talk to people about the subject of ministry or the term "full-time ministry," it is easy for people to have strange concepts. Christians enjoy the game of trying to figure out the answer to the question, "What is *my* ministry?" Or, perhaps even more, "What is *your* ministry?"

In this context, the word "ministry" has come to take on a super-spiritual ring to it. At times, older believers can intimidate the newer believers with the mystery of this spiritual quest to discover the answers.

The truth of the matter is that the word "ministry," as it appears in many translations of the Bible, simply means "service." Instead of asking, " What is my 'ministry?'" I should be asking, "What 'service' am I able to render to others that might be a strength and blessing to them?"

Who Is the Greatest?

Too many believers are jockeying for position and trying to determine who is the greatest in the kingdom of God. Too many people are looking for a position where they can sit and be served rather than looking for the towel or the apron of humility with which to wash the feet of others.

They are not unlike the twelve disciples of Jesus before the Holy Spirit supernaturally touched them. Early in their experiences, the disciples were self-motivated, jealous of each other and any other would-be leaders, and they were ambitious for power and placement in the kingdom that Christ would establish.

James and John epitomized this mentality when they came to Jesus and made a request for the chief seats in God's glorious kingdom, at the right and left hands of Jesus (see Mark 10:35-45). They wanted to sit on a throne. They wanted to rule. They wanted to sit and be served.

When the other disciples heard of the request that James and John had made, they were very displeased. Not because they felt that the attitude of James and John was poor and needed adjustment. They were upset because James and John got to Jesus first and there were only two such seats!

To Rule or To Serve

Something in the heart of the rest of the disciples wanted the same thing that James and John had desired. There is something in the heart of every man and woman that is equally selfish. We want position, power, or a name for ourselves; and we want to sit while others serve or minister to our wants.

Sometimes this is the way we approach the Lord Jesus Himself. When James and John approached Jesus, they said, *"Teacher, we want you to do for us whatever we ask"* (Mark 10:35). It is as if Jesus was their errand boy who was there primarily to tend to their wishes and desires. We call Jesus "Master," and then we want Him to do whatever we ask.

The disciples should have been asking, "Master, what do you want us to do? How can we serve and lay our lives down for you as you have been so willing to do for us?"

When Jesus sensed the motivation in the disciples' hearts, He knew it was time for one of His friendly chats. Jesus knew that if He were to build a church with this group of apostles, he would have to start with the first and most important thing—the motivation in their hearts.

1 Corinthians 14:

Ministry Equals Service

Jesus proceeded to talk to His followers and teach them about true ministry and true greatness. When you are called into the ministry, you are called into a life of service. If you want to be great in the kingdom of God, you must humble yourself, become like a little child, and become the servant of all. This was one of the major problems with the Pharisees of Jesus' day. The Pharisees had a lot of knowledge, but they loved the chief seats, titles, and the people's respect and homage. We are living in a day when many people are looking for a pecking order in the church. Many are not concerned about who can be the lowest or the chief servant. They are concerned about who is the greatest. What is the ultimate position that I can attain to in the church? Who has the highest rank?

Until we pay heed to Jesus' admonition to His disciples, we will not see a restoration of true apostolic ministry to the church. For many people, the apostolic ministry is that person of rank in the church to which they can hopefully aspire.

Until we can deal effectively with the desire for pre-eminence in the heart of man, we will not be able to accept the biblical definition of an apostle. If we are not careful, we will not want a true biblical definition, because it will not cater to our desire to rule and be great.

Servants First, Apostles Second

If we find out that the ministry of an apostle is a position that requires a death to the self, a life of humble service and sacrifice, and a willingness to be discredited for the sake of the Gospel, we might not be so eager to see it restored. An apostle is to be a servant above all things, as Jesus modeled to his disciples by washing their feet at the Last Supper (see John 13:1-17).

3

Paul understood what it meant to be an apostle. He realized that he was to be a servant first. In fact, he viewed it as more or less a sentence of death (see 2 Corinthians 1:9). He felt that apostles were last in God's succession of ministry (see 1 Corinthians 4:9). He indicated that they had been made out as "...*the filth of the world, the offscouring of all things until now*" (1 Corinthians 4:13). The path to Paul's vision fulfillment seemed to be one of suffering instead of glory.

Peter did not have any delusions of grandeur when it came to apostolic ministry either. Peter understood that he was a servant first and an apostle second (see 2 Peter 1:1). When he wrote to the elders of the church, he wrote as a <u>fellow elder.</u>

As you look over the church world today, there are many who are using the term "apostle" for their own ministry. Christian publications are filled with leadership conferences where apostolic ministers are present. In many cases they are using the term in a very scriptural way. Unfortunately, at times it also seems that there is a dangerous phenomenon taking place where the apostle appears to be elevated above the other ministries in the body of Christ.

People Want a King

Her to
person
worship.

People are always looking for a king. The children of Israel wanted a king like all of the other nations. People love to have an ultimate figure that they can place up on a pedestal and salute. The word apostle lends itself to this use (or abuse) because it has an authoritative sound to it. And since it is a word or concept that we do not fully understand in our culture, we can give it our own meaning and interpretation.

A few years ago the popular title was "bishop." The term "<u>bishop</u>," or more properly, "<u>overseer</u>," is a biblical term. In fact, Paul indicated that if you desire the office of a bishop, you desire a good work (see 1 Timothy 3:1). A bishop in New

Testament times was simply an overseer, or one of the elders of a local church (compare Titus 1:5 and 7). It was actually a description of the office an elder held—that of overseer to the church. Churches in the New Testament Era were led by groups of elders or overseers (bishops).

In our day, the term "bishop" is rarely used in this sense. It is more commonly used to apply to a pastor of pastors, a leader of a group of churches, a denominational supervisor, or any variety of other positions not specifically mentioned in the Bible. As a result, the word "bishop" has lost some of its original meaning. I hope this does not sound as if I am against the use of this title. I do think, however, it is important that we not create a spiritual hierarchy that unduly elevates one ministry above another.

Just as was the case with the term "bishop," the term "apostle" is not always currently used as the Bible defines it. In many cases, the term is being defined as a title of respect rather than a specific function or ministry. In some cases, unfortunately, the use of the term has highlighted man's quest for the ultimate ministry of a king.

The Gentile Way

Jesus made it clear that being motivated by a desire for preeminence was the Gentile way. The Gentile way involves hierarchy where people in authority lord it over those under their authority. He said it was not to be that way among His people.

A New Testament apostle was not a ruler among the people. The apostle was an important ministry that had a specific function. It is important that we work hard to discover what that function is supposed to look like. If God is indeed restoring this ministry to the church, we must have a biblical idea of what is being restored. We do not simply want the restoration of the title, we want a restoration of the ministry and function of the apostle.

If this is going to happen we must bring the ministry of the apostle into biblical focus. We must not turn to the Gentile way of forming ministry in the body of Christ—we must instead find our hierarchy in the Bible. Until we do this, we will be deprived of the function an apostle is to render to the body of Christ.

The Spirit of Christ

From a biblical perspective, Jesus represents the perfect example of apostolic ministry. Jesus must be our pattern for all ministry, and especially, for our purposes, all apostolic ministry. He has to be the one after which all those who feel called to an apostle pattern themselves. Jesus demonstrated His preeminence when He girded Himself with a towel and washed the disciples' feet (see John 13:3-5).

Jesus had to leave the earth physically, but He wanted His apostolic ministry to continue. When He ascended on high, he distributed the ministry that was in Him to human beings. To some He gave His ministry of teaching. To others He gave His ministry of prophecy. And to still others He gave His ministry as an apostle (see Ephesians 4:8-11).

What we long to see today is Jesus' ministry of an apostle. We are not interested in anything but authentic apostolic ministry. We want to see fathering servants. We want to see Jesus!

2

THE
WORD
"APOSTLE"

"And when it was day, He called his disciples to Himself; and from them He chose twelve whom He also named apostles."

(LUKE 6:13)

When Jesus gathered His disciples together after an all-night prayer meeting and named twelve of them apostles, He did not make up a new term (see Luke 6:12-16). He was not praying for a new title by which to call them. When Jesus called twelve of his followers apostles, He took a word that was already used in their culture.

One of the problems that we face in defining this ministry is that we have no cultural reference point for the ministry of an apostle. The average person living in the 21st century has never heard the word "apostle" used in their day-to-day life.

If Jesus had named twelve of his followers "plumbers," we would easily understand what he was saying because we are familiar with plumbers and the work that they do.

If Jesus had named these twelve "teachers," we would also have immediately understood what He meant. There are teachers in every culture. Because we have grown up with the concept of a teacher, the term does not need a detailed explanation. It is a function that we see all around us.

But Jesus did not refer to these twelve men as "plumbers" or "teachers," He called them "apostles." This is not a word or concept with which we are familiar. We cannot point to a representative in our culture and say, "that is an apostle."

Bridging the Cultural Gap

If we are going to understand this concept the way Jesus intended and if we are going to understand this appointment the way the disciples must have understood it, we need to understand the cultural history of this word.

It does not appear that the twelve disciples or the other people who heard Jesus make this appointment had a problem with the word. When Jesus named them "apostles," they did not say, "That's great Jesus, but what is an 'apostle?'" They understood what Jesus meant.

So what did the disciples hear when Jesus gave them this title? What was an apostle in Greek or Roman culture? What was the function? And how did it apply to these twelve men?

Unraveling the Mystery

The best way to bring some initial clarity to a ministry or function is to define the word or title itself. This works well for ministries like the evangelist which means, "a messenger of good news," or the pastor which means, "one who feeds or tends a flock." This method, however, does not help us much with the ministry of the apostle. When you translate and define the Greek word for apostle, you simply get, "one who is sent." This is so general that you could apply this definition to almost everybody and everything. In fact, I heard a speaker once try to define an apostle by looking up every reference in the Bible to someone or something being sent. By the time the speaker was finished, everyone seemed to be an apostle.

I do not think, however, that this is what Jesus had in mind when He appointed the Twelve. I do think He was somehow distinguishing these twelve from the rest of the other disciples or followers that He had by the use of this term.

Certainly there is a sense in which all ministries and all members of the body of Christ are supposed to be sent. Hopefully, we can all feel that we are ambassadors of the Lord with His commission, anointing, and blessing on our lives.

This word that Jesus used was both a general word and a very specific word. In its verb form, it simply means, "to send" and could be applied fairly generally to anyone or anything that was sent. But in its noun form, an apostle, or a "sent one," was a specific title that referred to a specific function.

In Greek Culture

The word "apostle" was originally a seafaring term that was most specifically applied to military expeditions. It at times referred to a fleet of ships and the officer that commanded the fleet.

As time went on, it came to be applied to a man or group of men who were sent out on an official expedition that was authorized by the government for a particular purpose. It carried the idea of authorization and commissioning by the higher power to act on the behalf of that power.

Its meaning grew even more specific over time as the Greeks, and later the Romans, sought to spread their cultural influence into all of the regions that had been conquered by their armies. In order to bring Greek or Roman rule to alien cultures, apostles would be authorized by the state and sent on an expedition with a fleet of ships filled with colonists. These colonists would then set up a model city or colony with a model culture in the newly conquered lands (see Acts 16:12). These colonies became regional centers from which Greek or Roman culture could be spread to the smaller cities and regions round about. In this way, those nations that had been physically conquered militarily could be conquered ideologically and culturally as well.

The focus of the word "apostle" was on two things: the pur-pose and the sender. An apostle was always someone sent out with a specific purpose or goal that in time could be specifical-ly measured. In addition, an apostle was always acting on behalf of the sender. In fact, in the history of this word, the focus is more on the sender, than on the one who is sent (see Isaiah 6:8). The apostle is a clearly commissioned and authorized agent of a higher power who is fully accountable to that power for the results of the mission that originates from that power.

An apostle later came to be an official ambassador or an emissary for a higher authority. As such, he was to be the embodiment and true representation of the sender. The sent one was to be absolutely faithful to the purposes and intentions of the sender. [1]

An Apostle is Accountable

Some people have an idea of apostolic ministry that is very loose. They somehow see the apostle as different from many of the other ministries in the body of Christ. While they acknowl-edge the fact that all of the ministries of the body of Christ function under local church authority, they see the apostle as free from direct personal accountability and yet one who holds others accountable.

This could not be further from the truth. In Greek society and culture, the apostle was a person who had a great deal of accountability to the person or persons who had sent and com-missioned him.

Paul was subject to personal accountability. He was sent from the Antioch church with a divine mission (see Acts 13:1-3). When he completed the mission, he returned and gave an account of his work (see Acts 14:26-28). When he was not on a missionary journey planting or following up on churches, he was home functioning on the local level with the rest of the leadership team in Antioch.

Peter was also subject to personal accountability. While in Jerusalem, it is clear that he fully recognized the authority and headship of the chief elder of the Jerusalem church—James (see Acts 12:17). Peter refers to himself in his day-to-day function as a fellow elder (see 1 Peter 5:1).

The very term "sent one" implies the concept of accountability. Who is over the apostle? To whom does the apostle answer? Who makes needed adjustments in the life and ministry of the apostle?

The answer is again found in the very meaning of the word. The apostle is accountable to the sender. "But who is the sender?" you may ask. "Is it God? Or is it a local church?" The truth is, it is both.

Called by God, Sent by Man

Certainly an apostle is a person who is first and foremost called by God. Paul made no apologies for that. He began most of his letters affirming the fact that he was called by God to be an apostle. But in reality, how is that different from any of the other ministries in the body of Christ? The pastor needs to be called by God to be a pastor. The teacher needs to be called by God to be a teacher. The exhorter needs to be called by God to be an exhorter. It is God that places the members in the body of Christ as it pleases Him (see 1 Corinthians 12:18).

In this case, we must separate calling from sending. All ministries are called by God. The apostle is a "sent one." In the case of the twelve disciples of Jesus, Jesus Himself sent them out two by two to go from city to city preaching and demonstrating the power of the kingdom of God wherever they went.

In Paul's case, hands were laid upon him by his covering church body in Antioch, and he was sent out with (perhaps even under) Barnabas to do the work to which God had called them. Paul did not go without the sanction and sending of the local church.

The truth is that there are two aspects of every person's ministry life. One deals with that ministry's relationship to God. The other deals with that ministry's relationship to human authority. In the kingdom of God, every member of the kingdom must submit his or her life to the King of the kingdom, the Lord Jesus Christ (see Acts 5:14). But those who are added to the kingdom or to Christ are also to be added to the church (see Acts 2:41,47).

Every believer is also to be subject to God's delegated authorities. This includes His authority that has been divested in parents and civil governments. But it especially applies to His authority that has been divested in the church. Not just the universal church (see Matthew 16:18-19), but to the local church (see Matthew 18:15-20). Every believer, no matter what ministry they may possess, must be submitted to *"those who rule over [them]"* in the local church (see Hebrews 13:17).

Those who rule over you, in God's mind, are not a hand-picked board of loosely related, sympathetic ministries who never really meet together or offer any serious financial, moral, or ethical accountability. In God's mind, those who have the rule over you are always the elders of a local church of which every believer should be a vital part.

There is no ministry that is not at the same time under God's rule and under local church rule. The senior pastor of a church may be the spiritual head of a given local church, but he or she is still under the authority of the eldership of that church. An apostolic ministry may have a strong mobile aspect to his ministry but he is still under the authority of the local church that sent him out.

When an apostolic ministry functions in a way that is out of character for a representative of Jesus, there should be a church leadership team that can be notified so that the appropriate steps can be taken. There is no other group of people authorized by Christ to carry the authority of the kingdom in the area of discipline other than the local church (see Matthew 18:15-20; 1 Corinthians 5:4-5).

Why is this so important? Because today there are self-appointed apostles who expect to be received as such, but are not under someone's authority, or in a true accountability relationship with a sending church. In essence, they are a law to themselves.

Since no ministry is infallible and invulnerable to the temptation to abuse and misuse their position, it is absolutely essential that all ministries submit fully to Christ's headship through the leadership team of their respective local churches.

If true apostolic ministry is to be received with confidence, we must know that they are called by God and sent by the church for the work that they are endeavoring to do. When this confidence is lacking, we will never experience the full benefit of this ministry to the Body.

To summarize, we can say that an apostle is a ministry with the spirit of Christ who is rightly related to heavenly and earthly authority. An apostle is called by God and sent by the local church to function in the present apostolic ministry of Jesus. An apostle is not over the church, but sent by a local church and accountable to that local church leadership team for the work that he or she is sent to do.

Not over the Church

3

JESUS—
THE APOSTLE
FROM HEAVEN

"Therefore, holy brethren, partakers of the heavenly calling, consider the Apostle and High Priest of our confession, Christ Jesus, who was faithful to Him who appointed Him, as Moses also was faithful in all His house." (HEBREWS 3:1-2)

If we are going to get a true biblical picture of what it means to be an apostle, we must first study the life and ministry of Jesus. Jesus Christ is the prototype for all apostolic ministry. When Jesus came to earth, He came as the Apostle from heaven. He was the Sent One of the Father. As such, He serves as the model for all apostolic ministry. All other apostolic ministries must measure themselves by Him.

Jesus, According to John

John, in his Gospel, seems particularly interested in presenting Jesus to us as the Apostle from heaven. In John, the emphasis is on Jesus' relationship to His Heavenly Father and the mission given to Him by His Father.

Over and over again we see all of the aspects of true apostolic ministry highlighted by John in the life of Jesus. Jesus was sent by the Father. He was sent as a representative of the Father. He was sent as a faithful representation of the Father. He spoke the words that were given to Him by the Father. He was sent out to establish a church. After His mission was accomplished, He returned to the Father.

Jesus — the Apostle Sent by the Father

It is clear in John's Gospel that Jesus did not come by His own initiative and by His own authority, but He was responding to the One who had sent Him. Arguably the most often quoted verse in the Bible highlights Christ's commissioning by the Father.

> *"For God so loved the world that he gave His only begotten Son, that whoever believes in Him should not perish but have everlasting life. For God did not **send** His Son into the world to condemn the world, but that the world through Him might be saved."* (JOHN 3:16-17, EMPHASIS MINE)

Notice some of Jesus' statements that John records (emphasis mine):

> *"But I have a greater witness than John's; for the works which the Father has given Me to finish—the very works that I do—bear witness of Me, that the Father has **sent** Me."* (JOHN 5:36)

> *"I am One who bears witness of Myself, and the Father who **sent** Me bears witness of Me."* (JOHN 8:18)

> *"I proceeded forth and came from God; nor have I come of Myself, but He **sent** Me."* (JOHN 8:42)

> *"As you have **sent** Me into the world, I also have **sent** them into the world."* (JOHN 17:18)

> *"Peace to you! As the Father has **sent** Me, I also send you."* (JOHN 20:21)

Jesus the Apostle Represents the Father

When Jesus came as the Apostle sent by the Father, He was not representing Himself. He was commissioned by the Father to do the work given to Him by the Father, and to minister the doctrine or teaching that the Father entrusted to Him. He was, in essence, the embodiment of the Father. When you saw Jesus, you saw the Father. If you rejected Jesus, you also rejected the Father.

This vital connection that Jesus had to the Father is very important if we are going to understand the ministry of an apostle. One of the key qualities of apostolic ministry is faithfulness. Jesus was faithful to the Father who had sent Him. He was faithful to represent Him fully. He was faithful to the plan that the sender had designed.

Notice again some of Jesus' own statements concerning His (the sent one's) relationship to His Father (the sender). Again, the emphasis is mine:

> *"Did you not know that I must be about **My Father's business.**" (LUKE 2:49)*

> *"My food is to do the will of Him who sent me and to finish **His work.**" (JOHN 4:34)*

> *"Most assuredly, I say to you, the Son can do nothing of Himself, but what He sees the Father do; for whatever **He does,** the Son also does in like manner." (JOHN 5:19)*

> *"He who does not honor the Son does not honor the Father who **sent** Him." (JOHN 5:23)*

> *"I can of Myself do nothing. As I hear, I judge; and My judgment is righteous, because I do not seek My own but the will of the Father who **sent Me.**" (JOHN 5:30)*

*"I have come in **My Father's name**...."* (JOHN 5:43A)

*"My doctrine is not Mine, but His who **sent** Me."* (JOHN 7:16)

*"He who speaks from himself seeks his own glory; but He who seeks the glory of the One who **sent** Him is true, and no unrighteousness is in Him."* (JOHN 7:18)

*"I have not come of Myself, but He who **sent** Me is true, whom you do not know. But I know Him, for I am from Him and He **sent** Me."* (JOHN 7:28B-29)

*"And He who **sent** Me is with Me. The Father has not left Me alone, for I always do those things that please Him."* (JOHN 8:29)

"I speak what I have seen with My Father...." (JOHN 8:38A)

*"I must work the works of Him who **sent** Me...."* (JOHN 9:4A)

"...believe that the Father is in Me, and I in Him." (JOHN 10:38B)

*"He who believes in Me, believes not in Me but in Him Who **sent** Me. And he who sees Me sees Him who **sent** Me...For I have not spoken on My own authority; but the Father who **sent** Me gave Me a command, what I should say and what I should speak."* (JOHN 12:44,45,49)

"He who has seen Me has seen the Father; so how can you say, 'Show us the Father'? Do you not believe that I am in the Father, and the Father in Me? The words that I speak to you I do not speak on My own authority; but the Father who dwells in Me does the works. Believe Me that I am in the Father and the Father in Me, or else believe Me for the sake of the works themselves." (JOHN 14:9B-11)

"He who does not love Me does not keep My words; and the word which you hear is not Mine but the Father's who **sent** *Me."* (JOHN 14:24)

"I came forth from the Father and have come into the world. Again, I leave the world and go to the Father." (JOHN 16:28)

Jesus — the Apostle as Church Planter

When studying the concept of the apostle in Greek and Roman culture, you will find that Jesus fits the model very well. Jesus was sent from a different culture (heaven) to extend that culture's rule to a new region (earth). He was sent by the Father to establish a church (see Matthew 16:18).

Jesus followed all of the principles of a good church planter when he came to the earth. He came with purpose. He knew that His Father's business was to establish the church and from the point that His official ministry began, He worked toward that end.

When Jesus came to earth, He identified with the culture that He came to reach. He learned the language and lived according to the lifestyle of the people that He came to reach.

He came with a mission. He came with no intention of staying. He came to establish His church and to return to the place from where He was sent. In doing this, He provided a pattern for us in the area of apostolic church-planting ministry.

Jesus — the Apostolic Church Planter

Every church planter should look at and study the ministry of Jesus in His task of planting the church. He modeled a methodology that was to be later followed by Paul and many others in the New Testament Age of church growth and expansion.

Jesus had a very simple plan that involved five main steps:

1. *EVANGELISM.* The initial focus of Jesus' ministry was to gather a following. He preached openly, in the streets and on the hillsides. He came to men where they were and preached to them the message of the kingdom. He invited them through repentance, water baptism, and a changed lifestyle to enter into the kingdom.

2. *DISCIPLESHIP.* Jesus soon began to focus His energies on a select group of followers who were more ready than others to forsake all for the call. He spent special times of training with these potential leaders communicating His values and ministry philosophy to them.

3. *LEADERSHIP DEVELOPMENT.* Jesus chose twelve from His many followers and disciples whom He named apostles. These would be the ones to whom He would give most of His attention. These would be the ones that He would groom to carry on His work after He retired from the field. He would develop them through systematic teaching and training experiences.

4. *DELEGATION OF AUTHORITY.* Jesus divested Himself in these apostles who would be used to do the real work of church planting. They would actually reap the harvest that Jesus had sown while He was among them. Jesus would accomplish His declared mission through them.

5. *FOLLOW-UP.* Jesus stayed in continual contact with these delegated leaders through the ministry of the Holy Spirit. Even though the work was now in their hands, He was ever ready to work with them on an ongoing basis to assist them in problem solving, counsel, and support.

It is interesting that Jesus was not particularly concerned about numbers in this process. He knew that if He was going to plant a church, raising up leaders was the first and foremost order of business. He knew that if He focused on leadership development, there would be sufficient leaders to take care of the people when the numbers did arrive.

Jesus — the Mentor of Leaders

Because of His apostolic mantle, Jesus was able to develop seasoned leaders after a few short years. Many leaders struggle to develop like-minded leadership. This was not a problem for Jesus. Jesus had great patience with those who felt the call of God on their life. He had an eye for those who had potential and He was willing to take the time and had the patience to work through the training process.

Jesus had success in leadership development because He had a five-pronged approach. First of all, He demonstrated for them what He expected of them. Leaders who are not willing to be a role model will never be successful in developing leaders. People need to see the word made flesh. This is why Paul

Model

service

was so successful. He was able to say, *"Imitate me, just as I also imitate Christ"* (1 Corinthians 11:1). Jesus demonstrated for His disciples how to minister to others. He never asked them to do something that He was not willing to do and had not demonstrated.

prayer

Second, Jesus spent much time in personal prayer for these followers. Not only did He let the Holy Spirit guide Him in making His initial selection (see Luke 6:12-16), He also prayed for their specific needs and ways to minister specifically to those needs (see Luke 22:32; John 17).

Third, Jesus had a specific training program for His followers. Training for ministry is not something that you merely catch by the process of osmosis (or to be more scientifically correct, diffusion). It is important to be around anointed ministries, but systematic instruction is still very important.

Fourth, Jesus taught them to function independently of Him. Some leaders make people overly dependent on them and their leadership. This has the effect of making followers like children who never grow up. Jesus knew how to release people by giving them the experiences necessary for confidence in future function in His absence.

Finally, Jesus opened doors of ministry opportunity for them. He sent them out two by two to try their wings and report back to Him. He sat down with them and evaluated their experiences by commending their successes and using their failures as a basis for further instruction (see Luke 9:1-5; 10:1-10, 17-20).

Jesus — the Shaper of Arrows

In all of Jesus' ministry, He was shaping arrows that could be shot out to hit a designated target (see Isaiah 49:1-2). Everything He did with these leaders He did with purpose in mind. He was training future apostles. His goal was that His followers would reach their full potential and realize the ministry to which they were called. What did He teach His prodigies? Jesus focused His teaching on eight primary areas:

1. *OBEDIENCE.* He taught them to live and minister in absolute obedience to the will of God, withholding nothing for self, but placing themselves entirely upon the altar.

2. *PRAYER.* He taught them the life and ministry of prayer in the Spirit (though they only entered it fully after the day of Pentecost).

3. *EVANGELISM.* He taught them how to meet people at their point of need and preach to them the message of the kingdom.

4. *SCRIPTURE.* He taught them how to know and use the Scripture. He taught them a love for the word of the Lord.

5. *FAITH.* He taught them to have faith in God directly for the supply of all their material needs. This accomplished four things: 1) It detached them from the world; 2) It obligated them to walk near to God; 3) It caused them to be living witnesses to God's power and faithfulness; and 4) It made them exercise faith.

6. *MINISTRY BY THE SPIRIT.* He taught them to minister in the power of the Spirit and not rely on ceremonies, programs, emotionalism, or any other human means to attract or influence.

7. *LOVE.* He taught them absolute love for their fellow man; the love that serves, seeking nothing for self, and counts it all joy and all gain to give all.

8. *TEAM MINISTRY.* He taught them to work together and cooperate as a group directed by the Holy Spirit of God. He taught them that their goal was not to seek the preeminence but to seek to serve one another.

Because Jesus was faithful and diligent to transmit and impart all of these things, His work would go on after He left. The Apostle, Jesus, had trained other apostles and church leaders who would be able to duplicate His ministry in the earth. The church that Jesus planted would succeed and transition from generation to generation.

Jesus is our model for all ministry in the body of Christ. It does not matter what ministry a person is called to do, it must be an extension of the ministry that was first demonstrated in the life of Jesus.

Jesus was The Apostle from heaven who was sent by the Father to establish a church. In doing so, He evangelized, developed a core group of leaders, mentored these leaders to carry out His vision, and eventually released them to function in His behalf.

The elements of apostolic function that we see in Jesus' life are accountability to a sender, evangelism, church planting, leadership training, mentoring, and releasing others into ministry. In other words, He was a fathering servant who lived for others. He was a faithful Son to the Father.

4

THE TWELVE APOSTLES OF THE LAMB

"Now the wall of the city had twelve foundations, and on them were the names of the twelve apostles of the Lamb." (REVELATION 21:14)

When Jesus, as the Apostle from heaven, came to earth to establish the church, He chose twelve of His disciples to become His apostles. This group of men would be His church-planting team and become the foundation for all subsequent church growth.

Many people do not recognize apostolic ministry today. They see the early apostles as a special group and react at the thought of expanding that group to include current ministries who function in the church today.

There is no question that these twelve men formed a special group of people. But they must be distinguished from all other apostles that follow. If we do not make such a distinction, we will miss what God wants to do through apostolic ministry today.

The early twelve were unique, first of all, because Jesus personally chose them in His earthly ministry (see Luke 6:12-16). Each call was unique, but they all had one thing in common: they were men of such disposition and persuasion that they were willing to leave all and follow Jesus.

The second thing that makes these twelve unique is that they have a unique set of qualifications. When the disciples felt the need to replace Judas, the fallen apostle, they enumerated what they felt were to be qualifications for his replacement. The main qualification was that his replacement had to be someone who had accompanied Jesus from His baptism in the Jordan to His ascension into heaven (see Acts 1:21-22).

The Twelve Apostles, Eternally Unique

There is no question that these twelve apostles were special in their day and they have been given a special place in the eternal plan of God. They are eternally unique for the following reasons:

1. *UNIQUE TITLE.* These twelve men are the only ones referred to as "apostles of the Lamb" in the Scripture (Revelation 21:14). While the word "apostle" is very common in the New Testament, this special title is reserved only for the Twelve. This is most likely an indication of their particular calling as cited above.

2. *UNIQUE FUNCTION.* These twelve men are one day going to be involved with Jesus in judging the twelve tribes of Israel (see Matthew 19:28). Whether or not these twelve tribes refer to the literal tribes of Israel is not certain. Most likely this refers to the Judgment Seat of Christ where the children of God are judged (see 2 Corinthians 5:10) as opposed to the Great White Throne judgment which is reserved for unbelievers (see Revelation 20:11).

3. *UNIQUE PLACEMENT.* These twelve men will find a unique placement in the twelve foundations of the Eternal City (see Revelation 21:14). This position is theirs most likely because their ministry was foundational to the establishing of not just the first local church, but the universal or mystical church, which is called the city of the living God (see Hebrews 12:22).

The Twelve Apostles, A New Order

When John the Baptist came to prepare the way for Jesus, he came as a transitional leader. He came at the end of one age and the inauguration of another.

"For all the prophets and the law prophesied until John."

(MATTHEW 11:13)

John stood at the end of the age of the law and the beginning of the age of grace. He separated the age of the prophets from the age of the apostles.

Throughout the history of God's dealings with man, God has used various instruments and vehicles to carry out His purpose. God began by using the patriarchs Adam, Noah and Abraham.

When the children of Israel came into the Promised Land, God used judges to be His instruments of deliverance to His people. They were used by God to call the people back to God and to lead Israel into victory over their enemies.

When Israel cried out for a king like all of the other nations had, a new age in Israel's history began. Samuel was a key figure here because he was the last of the judges, he anointed the first king, and he laid the foundation for a new order of prophetic ministry with his schools of the prophets. During the period kings ruled over the people of God, it was really the age of the prophets. It was the prophets who were God's mouthpiece to the kings to keep them on the right track. They were not always successful, but they were faithful to God as the purest ministry to function in the Old Testament. When John the Baptist came, he came as the last of this prophetic order. In fact, Jesus said that he was the greatest prophet to date (see Luke 7:28).

At this point, Jesus came on the scene and announced a new age. He declared His intention to build the church (see

Matthew 16:18) and the foundation of this church would be a new ministry that would be carried out by apostles. In doing so, He opened the door to the apostolic church age.

It is interesting that prophets wrote nearly all of the Old Testament books of the Bible. The New Testament writers, on the other hand, were primarily apostles. Together, these Old Testament prophets and the New Testament apostles, form the foundation of the new expression of God's purpose in the earth —the church (see Ephesians 2:19-22). The church today is the result of joining together the old order believers and the new order believers into one new establishment.

The Ministry of the Twelve

If all you ever discover about the twelve apostles of the Lamb you get from the New Testament (i.e. The book of Acts), you might consider them to be a rather inactive group of people. Some of the confusion comes in when we rely too heavily on the book of Acts, sometimes called the Acts of the Apostles.

It is important to understand that this title for the book of Acts is not the title given to it by the author of the book. I am not sure Dr. Luke would approve of that title. If you look at the book you will find that it is neither some of the acts of all of the apostles, nor all of the acts of some of the apostles. The book focuses primarily on two of the apostles, Peter and Paul. Peter is a key figure in the beginning, but the pictures taken from his life only serve to introduce us to Paul.

Many believe that Luke was writing a sequel to the Gospel that bears his name. They would see the book of Luke as an account of "Christ after the flesh," and the book of Acts as an account of "Christ after the Spirit."[2]

However, it is my contention that the book of Acts is not written about the twelve apostles of the Lamb at all, but is a biographical sketch of the life of Paul, possibly written by his good friend and traveling companion as a brief to file for Paul's upcoming trial before Caesar.[3]

If we are going to see the ministry of the Twelve, we have to go outside the pages of the New Testament to the annals of history for the complete testimony. When we look at history and reliable traditions, we see that these early apostles touched the then-known world and truly fulfilled Christ's charge to them in Acts 1:8.

While traditions regarding the early apostles are often conflicting and in no way hold the weight of the biblical accounts, they can be used to make one point: the twelve apostles did respond to the commission of Jesus and take the Gospel to much of the then-known world.

The following is a summary of some of the more reliable traditions regarding the extension of the Gospel by the twelve apostles of the Lamb. This information has been drawn from various Bible dictionaries.

1. Peter ministered in Jerusalem as a pillar in that church (see Galatians 2:9) and then became very mobile in his ministry. He spent time in Lydda, Joppa, Antioch of Syria, Rome, and Asia Minor. It is believed he was martyred under the reign of Nero.

2. John also began as a pillar in the Jerusalem church (see Galatians 2:9) but later, after the destruction of Jerusalem, moved to Ephesus. He became a key figure in the churches of Asia Minor and ministered a great deal in those regions until his exile on the isle of Patmos. When he died around A.D. 100, he became the only one of the Twelve to die of natural causes.

3. James the son of Zebedee, and the brother of John, was very close to Jesus and part of His inner circle (see Mark

5:37). He was the first of the Twelve to be martyred by Herod in about A.D. 42-44 (see Acts 12:1-2).

4. Andrew the brother of Peter is mentioned very little in the New Testament. However, tradition holds that he evangelized Scythia (the region North of the Black Sea). It is also a part of early tradition that he was martyred by crucifixion.

5. Philip, who was always listed fifth among the Twelve, is believed to have ministered primarily in the region of Asia Minor. There are many conflicting traditions as to Philip's manner of death, but most insist that he was martyred for his faith.

6. Thomas, who is sometimes distinguished among the Twelve because of his apparent doubt concerning Christ's resurrection from the dead, evidently overcame his doubts in a rather spectacular way. Thomas is believed by some to have been one of the greatest missionaries of all time. It is possible that he actually traveled east to India, and some believe as far as China, spreading the Gospel and planting churches. In fact, the only remaining church that claims to be founded by one of the Twelve is in India—a church supposedly planted by Thomas.

7. Bartholomew is another one of the Twelve about which very little is known. Some believe that he worked with Philip.

8. Matthew, who was also called Levi, seems to have worked primarily among the Hebrews seeking to reach them with the Gospel. His greatest achievement in relation to that endeavor is his authorship of the Gospel that

bears his name and is often referred to as the Gospel to the Jews. Later, it appears that his ministry expanded to Gentile peoples.

9. James the son of Alphaeus is another whose story is not well known. In the New Testament, he is only mentioned in the lists of the Twelve. The only reliable tradition is that he was stoned to death by the Jews for preaching Christ.

10. Simon, often referred to as the Zealot, is also given little attention in the pages of the New Testament. However, he is believed to have evangelized Libya in North Africa.

11. Thaddaeus, who is also named Judas the son of James, became a very active missionary. It appears that he was originally sent to Edessa, but because of persecution and threat of death, he pushed into other regions of the world establishing churches in present-day Iran and Western Afghanistan. He is also partly responsible for the Gospel reaching China in that first century.

12. Matthias is the disciple, presumably one of The Seventy, who replaced Judas Iscariot. Little is known of him. However, it is believed that he preached the Gospel primarily in Judea itself and died a martyr's death by stoning. Other traditions include Ethiopia as part of his sphere of influence.

The Apostolic Commission

It is clear as we look at this list of the twelve apostles of the Lamb that they took the commission Jesus gave to them seriously. Jesus met with them on several occasions after His resurrection and laid out the challenge to them (see Acts 1:2).

Christ's commission to them is summarized in five passages of Scripture, including Matthew 28:19-20; Mark 16:15-20; Luke 24:27; John 21:15 and Acts 1:8. His commission included several key elements:

1. *BEING WITNESSES.* The life and words of the Apostles were to bear witness to the Lord Jesus Christ. This witness was to be in word and in deed.

2. *PREACHING THE GOSPEL OR EVANGELIZING.* Wherever the early Apostles traveled, the Gospel was their key message, announcing the Good News of Christ which is the power of God unto salvation for the world.

3. *HEALING THE SICK.* The message that was entrusted to the early Apostles was for the whole man. The ministry of the early Apostles included signs, wonders, and mighty deeds.

4. *MAKING DISCIPLES.* This involved making sure that the foundation stones of repentance, faith, water baptism, Holy Spirit baptism, and coming under the Lordship of Jesus Christ were established in the life of every evangelized person (see Acts 2:38-40).

5. *PASTORING THE DISCIPLES.* Jesus made it clear that if a leader loves Jesus, then he will love His sheep. If a leader loves Jesus then he will feed (shepherd, pastor, tend to) the people of God to see that they come to a place of health and maturity.

6. *TEACHING THE DISCIPLES.* The command to the Apostles was to teach people to observe "all things" commanded by the Lord. Teaching would bring strength, establishment, and longevity to the churches that they would raise up.

In Acts 1:8, Jesus gave the Twelve a missionary strategy. They were to start in Jerusalem, move out to Judea, go on into Samaria, and finally go to the entire world with the Gospel. This is exactly what they did. The focus of Acts 2-7 is Jerusalem and Judea. In chapter 8, the Gospel moves into Samaria. From there it begins to spread to the whole world. The Apostles truly laid the foundation for the church, not just in doctrine, but in evangelistic endeavors.

We owe a great deal to this unique group of men that Jesus chose to initiate what we now call the church. They were the first ones to be given the title "apostle." They were men who centered their lives around the call of Jesus and risked everything to see the purposes of God realized in their lifetime.

Even though these twelve were a unique group, they were an example to apostles that would follow. After Christ's resurrection, He would inaugurate another order of apostolic ministry that would include the likes of Paul, Barnabas, Apollos and many others. This new order of apostles would build on what had been started by the Twelve and then continue to function until the return of the Lord when the church that was prophesied by Jesus is complete.

5

THE
APOSTLE PAUL
AND THE
TWELVE

"And He Himself gave some to be apostles, some prophets, some evangelists, and some pastors and teachers, for the equipping of the saints for the work of ministry, for the edifying of the body of Christ, till we all come to the unity of the faith and the knowledge of the Son of God, to a perfect man, to the measure of the stature of the fullness of Christ."

(EPHESIANS 4:11-13)

When you hear the word "apostle" there is no question that one of the main figures in church history that comes to your mind is the apostle Paul. Because of his huge place in the New Testament, including the biography of his life and work in the book of Acts, and his authorship of most of the New Testament epistles, he is sometimes considered to the be greatest of the apostles. In fact, on this basis, some have felt that Paul was God's choice to replace Judas among the twelve.

Not Judas' Replacement

It is critical that we do not see Paul as Judas' replacement. If Paul is seen as Judas' replacement then we do not have Paul's life as an example of what an apostle should look like in our day. It is my contention that Paul was not one of the Twelve, and I believe that this can be substantiated in a number of ways:

1. *PAUL DOES NOT QUALIFY AS ONE OF THE TWELVE.* If the qualifications listed in Acts 1 are indeed to be applied to those who qualify as a replacement for Judas, Paul falls short. Paul was not a companion of Jesus from His baptism by John to His ascension into heaven. In addition, Paul was not a witness of the physical resurrection of Jesus prior to His ascension.

2. *PAUL WAS NOT CHOSEN BY JESUS IN HIS EARTHLY MINISTRY.*
   Paul was called by Jesus after His ascension into heaven. That places Paul in the category of apostolic ministries that were given to the church, as described for us in Ephesians 4:7-11, upon the ascension of Jesus into heaven.

3. *THE TWELVE DID NOT CONSIDER PAUL TO BE ONE OF THEM.*
   Either you have to say that these twelve apostles had little or no spiritual discernment and that they were self-centered in their recognition of God's appointment, or you have to say the lack of recognition in relation to Paul was all part of God's plan to position Paul for his work among the Gentiles. There is no question from the language of Acts 1:17 that Matthias was *"numbered with"* the Twelve (also see Acts 6:2).

4. *PAUL DID NOT CONSIDER HIMSELF TO BE ONE OF THE TWELVE.*
   Paul makes references to the Twelve in his writings where he is obviously not including Judas Iscariot (see 1 Corinthians 15:3-5). Paul himself saw these men in a different category when he compared himself to them (see 1 Corinthians 15:9).

The reason why many feel that Paul was God's choice is, again, because of his prominent place in the New Testament and his foundational work in the church. There are several lines of argument given by those who assert that Paul was God's choice. They feel that:

1. *THE ELEVEN ACTED IN HASTE.* In Acts 1, the apostles are waiting together for the outpouring of the Holy Spirit that Jesus had promised them earlier. They were waiting in an atmosphere of prayer and in a spirit of obedience

to the Lord himself. As they prayed, they were quickened by the Holy Spirit through the reading of the Word of God that Judas' office was to be filled.

There is no indication of haste on their part and no other attempt by the Lord to intervene or annul this action on their part.

2. *CASTING LOTS WAS NOT AN APPROPRIATE WAY TO CHOOSE A REPLACEMENT.* While this is the only place in the New Testament where a decision was made in this manner, it must be remembered that the Twelve were still in essence functioning under the Old Testament form of guidance. In the Old Testament, God used external forms of guidance to speak to His people including such things as fleeces, Urim and Thummin and even the casting of lots (see Leviticus 16:7-10; Numbers 34:13; Joshua 14:2; Proverbs 16:33).

It should be noted that once the Holy Spirit was given to the church in Acts 2, this form of guidance was never used again. From that point on, the early believers would be led from within by the internal prompting of the Holy Spirit (see Acts 16:7).

3. *MATTHIAS IS NOT MENTIONED FURTHER IN THE NEW TESTAMENT.* If this line of argument were made, then we would have to eliminate most of the Twelve from the list of apostles. Where is Bartholomew? Where is Thaddaeus? Where is James the son of John? In actuality, very few of the Twelve are mentioned again in the New Testament.

This should not alarm us, nor should it give us reason to doubt anyone's apostleship. The fact is that the New Testament was never meant to provide a biographical sketch of the Twelve and their ministries.

There is, in point of fact, only one historical book in the New Testament, the book of Acts. And, as we have already pointed out, this is a book primarily about the life and ministry of one apostle, namely, the apostle Paul.

Everything written by Luke in the book of Acts seems to have direct bearing on one man – the apostle Paul. All of the events that Luke has selected to record seem to lay the groundwork for this apostle to the Gentiles.

4. *CHRIST PERSONALLY CHOSE PAUL IN ACTS 9.* While it is true that Christ personally chose Paul when He appeared to him on the road to Damascus, it is also true that this took place after Christ's ascension. Because of that, Paul would be categorized as an apostolic ministry that is separate from the Twelve.

Every ministry must be called by God. No matter where you function in the body of Christ, you should know that you are doing what you are doing because of the calling of the Lord.

Even if you equate this calling of Paul to Jesus choosing the original Twelve, you still must face the fact that Paul cannot meet the other qualifications for inclusion as a member of the Twelve. Also, if Matthias was one of the Seventy, as has been commonly supposed, he would have met the other qualifications.

Who Cares, Anyway?

What difference does it make anyway? Is this not just another one of those *"endless genealogies, which cause disputes rather than godly edification"* (1 Timothy 1:4)? Does this not become another exercise in futility?

Actually, this whole discussion makes a great deal of difference, especially when we want to discover the present day work and ministry of an apostle. If Paul is one of the twelve apostles of the Lamb, he cannot be an example or a pattern for us in our day of what an apostle is to be. You see, the twelve apostles of the Lamb have their own call, their own job description, and their own dispensation. As such, they cannot be a model for us because, as Apostles of the Lamb, there are twelve and only twelve.

However, Paul did refer to himself as a pattern of the New Testament believer (see 1 Timothy 1:16). Paul, I believe, actually became the first of a new order of apostolic ministry that Christ instituted upon His ascension into heaven.

Categories of Apostolic Ministry

In the New Testament, there are at least four categories into which we can place apostolic ministries. Each of these categories have specific qualifications and functions or ministries.

1. *CHRIST, THE APOSTLE FROM HEAVEN (SEE HEBREWS 3:1):* Jesus Christ was and is the Chief Apostle and the ultimate pattern against which all apostolic ministries must be measured.

2. *THE TWELVE APOSTLES OF THE LAMB (SEE LUKE 6:12-13):* This is a distinct group of apostles who were specifically chosen by Jesus during His earthly ministry. They have a unique place in all of eternity as those who laid the initial foundation of the eternal church.

   This group is used to reference a period of church history that is often referred to as the apostolic age of the church. Most church historians refer to the first one hundred years of modern history as the apostolic age, extending from the birth of Christ to the death of the last of the Twelve apostles (John) in or near the year A.D. 100.

Because that title is given to that period of church history some people have argued that the apostolic age is over and there are no more present-day apostles. This misunderstanding is based on an exaggerated emphasis on this historical title and a misunderstanding of the distinction between the twelve apostles of the Lamb and the post-ascension apostles.

3. *THE POST-ASCENSION APOSTLES:* Ephesians 4 tells us that upon His ascension into heaven, Jesus instituted a new order of apostolic ministry. This was the order of apostles that would function throughout the church age along with pastors, teachers, prophets, and evangelists.

This is the order of apostolic ministry to which the apostle Paul belonged. Paul was met on the road to Damascus by Jesus who, in His ascended state, called Paul to be an apostle to the Gentiles. Since this encounter followed Christ's ascension, Paul is a post-ascension apostle.

This order of apostolic ministry is to be a functioning part of the body of Christ that is given to build up and equip the church toward full maturity. This order of apostolic ministry is to be functioning throughout the church age *"till we all come to the unity of the faith and the knowledge of the Son of God, to a perfect man, to the measure of the stature of the fullness of Christ"* (Ephesians 4:13).

The New Testament mentions many apostles who fall into this category including:

Andronicus and Junia (see Romans 16:7).
James, the brother of the Lord (see Galatians 1:19).

Barnabas (see Acts 4:36; 13:2; 14:14).

Titus (see 2 Corinthians 8:23).

Epaphroditus (see Philippians 2:25).

Timothy and Silvanus (see 1 Thessalonians 1:1; 2:6).

Apollos (see 1 Corinthians 4:6,9).

This order of apostolic ministry is just as vital as any other part of Christ's Body, and without it functioning in its proper place, we will be lacking a vital ingredient in the equipping and perfecting of the church for its ultimate destiny.

4. *THOSE INVOLVED IN APOSTOLIC-TYPE MINISTRY:* In addition to the above categories, there seems to be quite a number of people in the New Testament who performed apostolic-type functions at times who were not specifically called apostles. Probably the best example of these are The Seventy who Christ sent out to do basically what the Twelve have been commissioned to do.

This seems to answer the question about many in our day who have been instrumental at some times and in some ways that might seem to be apostolic in nature and yet do not appear to be specifically called to that life ministry.

Paul Begins a New Order

The reason it is so important to make the distinction between these different categories of apostolic ministry and differentiate Paul from among the Twelve is that Paul serves as an example of the new order of apostolic ministry given to us by Christ for the present day. If Paul is not our example of apostolic ministry for today, then we do not have a good example to follow. But if Paul is to be that example, then we have some concrete guidelines for this ministry that define how it is to function in the body of Christ today.

Apostolic Ministry Continues Today

Many have tried to convince us that there are no more apostles and prophets in the church today. They will cite certain passages of Scripture and manipulate them to confirm a preconceived viewpoint. It seems we are often trying to equate our interpretation of the Scripture with our own present understanding and personal experience rather than allowing Scripture to speak for itself and then seek to match our experience to that. Especially when it comes to areas of the supernatural, there seems to be a tendency to put such things into the ages of the past. It can be done in order to avoid comparing ourselves to the biblical standard. It is an easy way to explain why we are not personally experiencing certain biblical truth.

However, we should be operating in just the opposite way. If we see something in the Bible that we are told can be part of our experience and we are not experiencing it, it should drive us to seek God for that biblical experience. In this way we can bring our experience up to the level of the Word.

This would apply to spiritual things like deliverance, healing, miracles, and all of the supernatural gifts of the Holy Spirit. It should also apply to every single ministry mentioned and described for us in the book of Acts.

It is important that we do not use faulty biblical interpretation to eliminate certain unfamiliar or even abused elements from our expression of Christianity. In doing so we can cut ourselves off from the things we need to reach the ministry goals that God has put in our hearts.

At times, people have used passages like 1 Corinthians 13 to deal with the issues of speaking with other tongues and prophecy. In this passage it indicates that these things are in some way incomplete or imperfect and they will cease when *"that which is perfect has come"* (verse 10).

However, while they may use this verse to eliminate tongues or prophecy, they never in any way suggest that at the same time we should eliminate knowledge which is put in the same category as those things that will *"vanish away"* (verse 8).

The point is that because all of these things function through imperfect vessels, they are all limited. In addition, they are further limited when they function without a spirit of love, which should be the motivation for all expressions of gifts and ministries in the church.

Some suggest that the "perfect" which is to come is the canon of Scripture. Yet we know that the best way to interpret unclear passages is from the clear passages.

Ephesians 4 tells us the time frame for these ministries and what the "perfect" is to be. These ministries are given by Christ *"till we all come to the unity of the faith and of the knowledge of the Son of God, to a perfect man, to the measure of the stature of the fullness of Christ"* (Ephesians 4:13).

I dare say that this has not happened yet, and will not happen unless the leadership ministries that are given to help make this a reality are fully functioning as Christ intended. We have no right to say to this part of the body or any other part of the body *"I have no need of you"* (1 Corinthians 12:21).

Seeking the True

If, then, the ministry of the apostle is to continue until Christ's return, we must cease from discussing whether or not this ministry is to exist in the church today and turn our attention onto how it is to function. We must turn our attention from trying to justify our past position and understanding concerning apostles and begin contending for the true biblical expression of this ministry.

We must also turn our attention away from the way in which we have seen this biblical title abused by those who have claimed to be apostles and not let that cloud or dampen our desire to see the true expression of this ministry released to the body of Christ. The counterfeit cannot be allowed to dampen our enthusiasm for the true.

In Paul, we now have a true example of how this ministry of the apostles should look in our day. Paul is not one the twelve apostles of the Lamb, he is an apostle chosen by Christ after His resurrection into heaven. As we turn our attention to his life, we will see the work and ministry of a true fathering servant to the church.

6

PAUL'S PATTERN

"However, for this reason I obtained mercy, that in me first Jesus Christ might show all longsuffering, as a pattern to those who are going to believe on Him for everlasting life."

(1 TIMOTHY 1:16)

Paul serves as the pattern for apostolic ministry in our day. We do not have to be bound by the qualifications and restrictions of apostolic ministry under the twelve apostles of the Lamb. Today, apostolic ministry is a post-ascension ministry that will continue to function until Christ's return. If Paul is our example, it is important to glean as much as we can from his life.

Paul an Unlikely Choice

Paul was both a likely candidate and an unlikely candidate to be a church-planting apostle. He was an unlikely candidate because of his initial posture concerning Christ and the church. Of all of the people alive in his day, Paul may have been the most vehemently opposed to the new Christian movement and felt that he owed it to God to stamp it out before it got off the ground. In reading Paul's own account of his pre-conversion testimony (remember Luke got his material from Paul himself), it is clear that he was intensely opposed to the followers of Christ.

The book of Acts describes Saul of Tarsus as actively involved in the death of the first martyr, Stephen (see Acts 7:58; 8:1). In addition, he wreaked havoc on the church (see Acts 8:3), was continually breathing threats and murder against the disciples (see Acts 9:1), and was exceedingly enraged against them (see Acts 26:11). He was zealous to see Christianity destroyed.

When Paul gave testimony to his actions concerning this time in his life, he indicated that he *"persecuted this Way to the death, binding and delivering into prisons both men and women"* (Acts 22:4). He further added that he *"punished them often in every synagogue and compelled them to blaspheme"* and when they were put to death, he *"cast [his] vote against them"* (Acts 26:10-11).

When Paul wrote to the Philippians, he indicated that when it came to persecuting Christians, he was zealous or "red-hot" (see Philippians 3:6). He held nothing back. Perhaps this is one of the things that Paul said he had to put behind him to move forward in the calling of God (see Philippians 3:13-14).

It is not difficult to understand why Ananias was so hesitant to pray for Saul's restored sight (see Acts 9:13-14). Or that the apostles and leaders of the Jerusalem church were initially so suspicious of Saul (see Acts 9:21,26). In fact, it can be argued that Paul was never fully accepted into the fellowship of the Jerusalem leaders.

As unlikely as this seems, God chose Paul to be an apostle and a preacher (see 1 Timothy 2:7). Paul gives us a clue into this apparent contradiction when he wrote to Timothy.

"And I thank Christ Jesus our Lord who has enabled me, because He counted me faithful, putting me into the ministry, although I was formerly a blasphemer, a persecutor, and an insolent man; but I obtained mercy because I did it ignorantly in unbelief." (1 TIMOTHY 1:12-13)

Paul, a Likely Choice

When you look at Paul from another angle, he was a perfect choice to be an apostle. Paul was not boasting when he wrote that he was, *"circumcised the eighth day, of the stock of Israel, of the tribe of Benjamin, a Hebrew of Hebrews; concerning the law, a Pharisee, concerning zeal, persecuting the church; concerning righteousness which is in the law, blameless"* (Philippians 3:5-6).

Paul was perhaps one of the most educated people of his day in both Jewish law and natural affairs, having studied under the tutelage of Gamaliel, one of the most respected educators of the day (see Acts 22:3). Many believe that Paul was being groomed for leadership in the Sanhedrin, or Jewish Council.

In addition, Paul had acquired a very portable trade that would be very handy to him as he traveled in ministry at the leading of the Holy Spirit. God would use this tent-making skill to help fund his missionary work and the work of the others.

Paul's Call

Perhaps it was because of this background that Paul seemed to always feel the need to justify his ministry as that of an apostle. If Paul had allowed negative voices or the acceptance or rejection of others to determine his ministry, he never would have made it out of Tarsus. Paul had to know that he was doing what he was doing by the calling of God.

Paul knew that it was God who had called him to be an apostle. He was not an apostle because his school guidance counselor told him that his natural skills matched with apostolic work. He was not an apostle because a ministry placement committee got together with him and helped him discover his hidden talents. He was not an apostle because a particular man or a group of men laid hands on him. Paul knew he was an apostle because of what Christ had done in him (see Galatians 1:1; 2 Corinthians 1:1; Titus 1:1).

As far as Paul was concerned, his being an apostle was not up for debate. He was called by God to be an apostle and, therefore, he had been given the faith and grace necessary for that work (see Romans 1:5; 12:3; Galatians 2:8-9). In addition, he knew that his particular function involved ministry to the Gentiles (see Romans 11:13).

Paul's Preparation

In spite of Ananias' glowing prophecy in relation to Paul when he was converted (see Acts 9:15-16), the doors of opportunity did not swing open wide for him very quickly. Even though Paul had some excellent credentials in the natural realm, he still had to graduate from the school of the Spirit before he was ready to be released into his call.

As you study the life of Paul, it is apparent that he spent from 10-13 years secluded in Tarsus and Arabia (compare Acts 9:20-30 with Galatians 1:11-24).[4] We do not know all that occurred during these years, but Paul undoubtedly experienced what Joseph experienced when the *"word of the Lord tested him"* (Psalm 105:19).

Like Joseph, he had the word of the Lord and a vision that had been implanted in his heart, but no one else seemed to see it. Similar to what Joseph experienced, everyone was suspicious and questioned Paul's motivation for ministry. And like Joseph when he shared his dream with his family, perhaps there was an element of pride in Paul. When you read Paul's testimony concerning himself you sense that he could have had a problem with boasting and pride at one time in his life. He comes close to sounding like he is boasting on a couple of occasions, but doesn't as he ultimately gives God glory for the work of grace in his life (2 Corinthians 11:16-33; Philippians 3:5-7). Perhaps God was dealing with this stronghold in Paul's life during these hidden years. All we know is when God was through with Paul, he was a fit vessel for the Master's use. His motives were refined to the place where he could say to the Ephesian elders:

" I have coveted no one's silver or gold or apparel. Yes, you yourselves know that these hands have provided for my necessities, and for those who were with me. I have shown you in every way, by laboring like this, that you must support the weak. And remember the words of the Lord Jesus, that He said, 'It is more blessed to give then to receive.'" (ACTS 20:33-35)

And again to the Thessalonians:

"For our exhortation did not come from error or uncleanness, nor was it in deceit. But as we have been approved by God to be entrusted with the gospel, even so we speak, not as pleasing men, but God who tests our hearts. For neither at any time did we use flattering words, as you know, nor a cloak for covetousness—God is witness. Nor did we seek glory from men, either from you or from others, when we might have made demands as apostles of Christ. But we were gentle among you, just as a nursing mother cherishes her own children."
(1 THESSALONIANS 2:3-7)

Whatever the case, preparing to be an effective ministry for the Lord involves more than an education. It also involves being emptied of pride and other ambitions that would get in the way of effective ministry for God.

Paul may have been forgotten by men, but he was not forgotten by God. There was a day when his word came and along with that a knock on the door from a man named Barnabas (see Acts 11:25-26).

Paul's Sending

Paul worked with Barnabas for a few years by helping to lay the spiritual foundation for the church at Antioch through his teaching. Ironically, this church was actually started by Paul in an indirect way. During the days of Paul's persecution of the church, the Christians in Jerusalem fled to other regions to avoid Paul's grasp. As these scattered believers shared their faith with others and people responded by coming to the Lord, churches were spontaneously established. One of these places was Antioch.

When the apostles in Jerusalem heard about these converts in Antioch, they sent Barnabas to bring order to what was going on and develop this evangelistic movement into a church (see Acts 11:19-26). With Paul's assistance, Antioch soon became a great church and a pattern to many churches for its missionary spirit and apostolic vision.

Paul's function in Antioch was not his ultimate calling, but it would be a wonderful training ground for him. In assisting Barnabas, Paul helped a man who believed in him to raise up one of the great churches of the New Testament Era. Paul had a terrific opportunity under the tutelage of a senior ministry to begin to hone his gifts and develop his teaching ability.

It was not long before Barnabas and Paul had reproduced themselves in others. This group of loosely related believers had become a strong church with other prophets and teachers (see Acts 13:1). Now Barnabas and Paul were able to step back and let others lead. When that happened, they were ready for the next phase of their spiritual journey.

During a special time of fasting, prayer, and waiting on God (see Acts 13:1-3), the Holy Spirit spoke again to Barnabas and Paul (undoubtedly through the prophetic ministries that were present). It was the time for Paul's original word from Ananias to come to pass and the official sending to take place. Paul would enter into the full function of a "sent one" (i.e. apostle). Paul had been called to be an apostle as a much younger man (possibly at around 30 years of age), now he was to be sent forth with that authority many years later (now about 45 years old!).

Paul's Work

Paul's slow start, as it were, would in no way limit his ability to be an extremely productive and effective ministry. The truth is that many ministries try to launch out before they are really ready. It seems you can either grow up and be sent out, or you can be sent out first and grow up later. It is better to follow the example of Paul where you can be proven and trained in the context of the local church and under the tutelage of senior ministries before you go out.

Once Paul got started, he did not let any grass grow under his feet. In the space of about 20 years (4 of which he was held prisoner), he traveled to over 100 cities, preached in at least 30 cities and established at least 10 strong, reproducing churches. Paul seemed to have known his purpose, and he performed it with a passion. Perhaps he felt he needed to make up for lost time. More than likely he was gripped with the lost condition of the people of the world and their need to experience the love of God in Christ Jesus (see 2 Corinthians 5:14).

Paul also seemed to have known how to perform his apostolic function with a sense of purpose. Perhaps it was his Roman background or familiarity with Greek culture that was handed down to him by Gamaliel. Whatever the case, he followed the pattern of both the Greeks and the Romans in the conquering of new territories. He had a basic, twelve-step methodology that he nearly always followed.

1. *HE MINISTERED IN TEAMS.* Paul was never intentionally alone in his apostolic work. Just as Jesus sent out the

twelve and the seventy two-by-two, Paul tried to function within this principle. Paul's main ministry gift, apart from that of an apostle, appears to have been that of a teacher. It is interesting that when he is teamed up with others, he is linked with those who seem to have more of a prophetic gifting (e.g. Barnabas and Silas, see Acts 15:32). This, of course, is a great principle for building a team. In making a balanced team you want ministries that complement each other and make up what is lacking in the other.

In addition to this, Paul always took a minister in training with him; not just to help carry his bags, but to watch, learn, and eventually minister right along side of him (e.g. Timothy, Titus, John Mark). Paul was always training others to do what he did.

2. *HE FOCUSED ON CHIEF CITIES.* Paul had several ways of determining exactly where to go and how to focus his ministry energy. First of all, he followed his natural reasoning. He knew he had a call to plant churches and there were a lot of places that needed churches to be planted. He could go almost anywhere and have the blessing of God.

Paul's second missionary journey began with a conversation between Paul and Barnabas about going back to visit the churches they had planted on their first trip (see Acts 15:36). When they completed the visits to those places they planned to go into Bithynia because that was the next natural step from where they had gone on his first missionary journey. It was then that the Holy Spirit arrested them and redirected them to Macedonia (see Acts 16:7-10).

Secondly, Paul focused on the places where the Holy Spirit seemed to be moving. Again he followed the instructions Jesus gave His disciples to not focus on places where they were rejected, but to preach where they were welcomed. If one city does not receive you, shake the dust from your feet and go to the next city. There are plenty of open places to preach.

Where is the Holy Spirit moving? Where are converts coming to the Lord in numbers? Where does the Spirit of the Lord seem to be stirring the waters? Send leadership to those places, much like the Jerusalem church did when they sent out Barnabas. In this way you minister to the prepared people.

This does not mean that you would never send apostolic ministry to hard areas. Hard areas would come under the guidance of a direct word from the Lord. If God specifically calls you to any place you must go.

Thirdly, Paul followed the direct leading of the Holy Spirit. When he was attempting to go into Bithynia, the Lord gave Paul a vision that changed his direction. Paul saw a man from Macedonia who pleaded with the apostle, "Come over to Macedonia and help us!" Paul immediately set his other plans on hold and followed what he believed to be the clear directive of the Holy Spirit (see Acts 16:9-10).

Finally, Paul focused on chief cities. When Paul got his call to Macedonia, he got the call to a large region. Macedonia is a region and not a city. So where do you go? You do what Paul did. You enter Macedonia, travel quickly through the smaller towns until you come to Philippi, *"the foremost city of that part of Macedonia"* (Acts 16:12).

Paul was following the Greek and Roman pattern and the pattern of Jesus when He came to Jerusalem. It was not that Paul had no vision for the smaller towns. In fact, it was his vision for the smaller towns that drove him to the larger ones. He knew that you can reach the small towns from the large towns as he proclaimed to the Thessalonians, but that it is very difficult to reach a large city from the beachhead of a small town.

"And you became followers of us and of the Lord, having received the word in much affliction, with joy of the Holy Spirit, so that you became examples to all in Macedonia and Achaia who believe. For from you the word of the Lord has sounded forth, not only in Macedonia and Achaia, but also in every place." (1 THESSALONIANS 1:6-8A)

3. *HE PREACHED OPENLY TO ALL.* Paul did not need an invitation to speak. He went looking for invitations and open doors that were available to him. He would speak to a crowd or to a single individual. He would speak in the marketplace, on a crowded street corner, in a synagogue, in a prison house, or on Mar's Hill. He believed God for divine appointments—supernatural encounters with prepared people.

4. *HE GATHERED A NUCLEUS.* Paul gathered people together who had responded to his preaching. He would work intensely with these people so that when he left, or was forced to leave, there would be a core of people who understood the message and had a strong commitment to each other.

5. *HE TAUGHT INTENSELY.* The focus of Paul's work with this nucleus was discipleship and teaching. He was, in essence, fulfilling the commission of Jesus to make disciples. As such, he focused first on repentance and turning to the Lord. This involved making sure that these followers experienced a proper Christian birth with

repentance, the true fruits of repentance, water baptism, the baptism of the Holy Spirit, and a separated lifestyle.

From there, Paul would focus on teaching. In Antioch both he and Barnabas spent two intense years teaching the people. The fruit of that teaching was a quality of Christianity that could truly be labeled "Christian" (see Acts 11:26). In other places, like Ephesus, Paul would use a facility like the school of Tyrannus for daily instruction in an attempt to teach these new converts to observe all things that Christ had commanded (see Acts 19:9; Matthew 28:20).

6. *HE TRAINED LEADERS*. Because Paul knew that his days were numbered in every city that he visited, he needed to train others to replace him. If he was going to leave an autonomous church in that city, training leaders was a major priority.

Paul was following the example of Jesus who had come to build a church. He was not too concerned whether or not he had a large group of people. The crowds would eventually come. He was concerned about a few good men and women who would be able to function as faithful leaders when he left.

Because of the circumstances surrounding Paul's life and ministry, because he always stirred up a hornet's nest and had people chasing after him, he often had to leave before he would have liked. But because he was so diligent about training, equipping, and releasing leaders, churches sprang up wherever he went.

7. *HE SET IN A PROVISIONAL LEADERSHIP TEAM*. When it was time for Paul to leave a new work either by his choice or by the given circumstances, he left the church in the hands of a provisional leadership team. At that point he

did not set in official elders for any of the churches. He set in leaders who could function in his absence and on his behalf.

8. *HE LEFT THEM FOR A SEASON.* Paul now left these fledgling churches to fly on their own. He went on to the next challenge before him and left this leadership team to function on his behalf. This was a proving time for these leaders. They were going to learn things on the job that they never could have learned in the classroom.

9. *HE RETURNED TO BRING ADJUSTMENT.* After a season of time (up to two years), Paul came back to this church to see how they were doing. He now focused on encouragement for the believers and any need for adjustment among the leadership that had been exposed in his absence (see Acts 14:22).

10. *HE SET IN ELDERS.* On this follow-up visit, they called the church together in a time of fasting and prayer. In this context, they officially set in elders and, in a sense, officially turned the work over to the Lord and His working through this new team of elders (see Acts 14:23). This now was an autonomous church.

11. *HE LEFT AGAIN.* Paul left this established church to function on its own. His relationship had now changed. Up until this time he had been the father of this work. He was the spiritual father of the leadership team and the authority or covering for the church. Now that the eldership was in place, Paul was still a spiritual father, but his lines of authority changed.

It is much like the authority that parents have in the lives of their children. When the children are in the home and under the direct authority of their parents, there is a chain of command that the children must acknowledge. However, when those same children get married and establish a home of their own, the relationship to their parents changes. Their parents are still their parents in a biological sense, but now the relationship changes to a chain of counsel rather than a chain of command.

Hopefully the relationship will always be strong and the children will always seek the counsel and advice of their natural parents, but now they are not necessarily required to follow it. This is a difficult change to make for parents. It is difficult to let one's children go to function on their own.

It was likely difficult for Paul at times. He was the one who had started these churches and sometimes he witnessed them going in directions that he would not have gone. It was especially hard when his own sons and daughters in the faith rejected his advice and counsel. But that experience is all part of the life cycle. It is true in the natural family and it is true in the spiritual family. Authority in anyone's life is based on relationship.

12. *HE FOLLOWED UP ON THEM.* Paul did not leave these churches totally on their own to fend for themselves. Even though he did not have the modern telecommunications network that we have at our disposal, he did the best that he could. He made follow-up visits. He sent some of his companions in ministry to visit on his behalf. In addition, he followed up through letters for which we are truly thankful. His follow-up mail has been a great encouragement to all of the churches that have followed in his faith.

Paul's Fruit

No one would ever question whether or not Paul was an apostle. The reason it is easy to see him as an apostle is because he had apostolic fruit. What kind of fruit did this tree produce? It produced strong churches that lasted for centuries to follow. It produced strong church leaders who continued to prosper after Paul's death. It produced a legacy of practical, pastoral doctrine that is still guiding and enriching the church of the twenty-first century.

Too often in our day people want to be recognized as apostles even though they have little or no apostolic fruit. Often, people become very vocal about a title that they desire for their ministry. I heard one man say once, "You don't have to hang a sign on an apple tree to tell you what kind of tree it is. Just wait until the time for the fruit. The fruit will reveal the type of tree that it is. An apple tree will produce apples!"

Paul was an apostolic ministry. He was a fathering servant who had apostolic fruit. The fruit of his ministry was strong believers, strong leaders, and strong churches. To Paul, the word "apostle" was a function, not a title. He knew what he was to do and he had developed a personal strategy to do it. He never introduced himself as "The apostle Paul," he let the work speak for itself. It was his relationship with those he served that gave him authority in their lives.

7

APOSTOLIC WORK

"Who then is Paul, and who is Apollos, but ministers through whom you believed, as the Lord gave to each one? I planted, Apollos watered, but God gave the increase. . .For we are God's fellow workers; you are God's field, you are God's building. According to the grace of God which was given to me, as a wise master builder I have laid the foundation, and another builds on it."

(1 CORINTHIANS 3:5-6, 9-10)

There are many people who may desire the title of apostle; but I wonder how many people desire the actual work of an apostle. I heard a great man once say, "There are many people after my position, but there are not nearly so many after my work."

What did he mean? He meant that it is easy to want a certain title, but it is another thing to actually desire the work that is required by that title. Perhaps this is what Paul meant when he said, *"If a man desires the position of a bishop, he desires a good work"* (1 Timothy 3:1).

Eldership is first and foremost a work. It is one thing to want to be called an elder or bishop. It is quite another thing to desire the work that goes with that position. It is one thing to enjoy being spoken to in respectful terms. It is another thing to desire to pastor people: to reach out and encourage the needy, patiently minister to the weak and hurting, and to lay your life down for the people of God.

Apostleship is a Work

Like eldership, being an apostle is first and foremost a work. Paul himself indicated that his life calling was not an easy path to walk. He even indicated that he worked harder than anyone else did (see 1 Corinthians 15:10). When you read some of Paul's comments concerning his ministry journey, it is difficult to envy his life's work (see 2 Corinthians 6:4-10; 11:23-29).

You might be wondering, what exactly is the work an apostle does? There is no specific job description for an apostle in the New Testament. While a study of the life and ministry of those called apostles will display a great deal of variety, there are some things that seem to be consistent in the ministry or work of all of the apostles.

Spiritual Fathers

Perhaps the key to understanding the ministry of an apostle is the word "father." Paul said that while *"you might have ten thousand instructors in Christ, yet you do not have many fathers"* (1 Corinthians 4:15). While Paul never married and had no natural children, he did see himself as the spiritual father of the Corinthian church. In his life and ministry he would have many spiritual sons and daughters.

Being a spiritual father begins with having the heart of a father. Paul had this heart. Sometimes when we read the writings of Paul, we can get the impression that Paul was a hard-hearted man who always had a bone to pick with people. This could not be further from the truth. In actuality, Paul had a very soft heart for those that God had placed under his spiritual care. He was jealous over them with a godly jealousy (see 2 Corinthians 11:2).

Paul allows us see to his heart when he writes to the Thessalonian believers:

> *"For our exhortation did **not come** from error or uncleanness, nor was it in deceit. But as we have been approved by God to be entrusted with the gospel, even so we speak, **not** as pleasing men, but God who tests our hearts. For **neither** at any time did we use flattering words, as you know, nor a cloak for covetousness—God is witness. **Nor** did we seek glory from men, either from*

you or from others, when we might have made demands
*as apostles of Christ. But we were **gentle** among you, just*
***as a nursing mother** cherishes her own children. So,*
***affectionately longing** for you, we were well pleased to*
impart to you not only the gospel of God, but also our
*own lives, because **you had become dear** to us. For you*
remember, brethren, our labor and toil; for laboring night
and day, that we might not be a burden to any of you, we
preached to you the gospel of God.

You are witnesses, and God also, how devoutly and
justly and blamelessly we behaved ourselves among you
who believe; as you know how we exhorted, and comfort-
*ed, and charged every one of you, **as a father** does his*
own children, that you would walk worthy of God who
calls you into his kingdom and glory."

(1 THESSALONIANS 2:3-12, EMPHASIS MINE)

Here Paul makes it clear that he had the people of God in
his heart and his ministry to them was not selfish on his part.
His motives were not impure. He was not in ministry for what
he could get out of it. He was not interested in their money,
their praise, or their veneration. In fact, just to prove it, he did
not take money from them, but worked with his own hands to
support himself while he was with them.

Paul did not want there to be any confusion on this point.
Even though as the father of the work and the founding ministry he could have organized things to his personal advantage,
what he did among them was pure, upright, and always in
their best interest.

Paul compared himself to a nursing mother who is gentle
with her newborn child. The mother is willing to give over her
life and schedule for the sake of this new child who has come
into the world. She is ready to do whatever is necessary for the
child to have the best possible start it can have.

Paul was like a nursing mother who has given birth to this church in Thessalonica. That church was like a newborn baby. Paul said that he took similar care and nurture with them so that they could have a healthy start as a church. He only did what was in the best interests of the church.

Paul further stated that he ministered to them like a father does to his own children. Paul viewed people as his spiritual children. He possessed a sense of responsibility to see them become mature and function effectively on their own. Paul did what he did among them because he genuinely cared for them.

The Father's Heart

If apostolic ministry is going to be effective, it must spring from a heart that is like that of Paul. It must spring from a love for the church and the purposes of God. It must spring from a father's heart that puts others ahead of self, is willing to become poor so that others can become rich, and is willing to get intimately involved with both the successes and failures of those under its charge.

1. *A HEART OF LOVE:* Often when we think of love, we think of mothers instead of fathers. Yet in the Bible, it is clear that God's model of a father is that of love. Just like the heavenly Father, the natural father is to be the source of love in the home. True love puts others ahead of self and is described in detail in 1 Corinthians 13:

   "Love suffers long and is kind, love does not envy; love does not parade itself, is not puffed up; does not behave itself rudely, does not seek its own, is not provoked... bears all things, believes all things, endures all things. Love never fails." (VERSES 4-5,7-8A)

2. *A HEART OF SELF-SACRIFICE:* The love of the heavenly Father is a giving love (see John 3:16). A true father is always willing to put the needs of others ahead of his own. There are many selfish fathers, but that is not God's heart. The true father lays his life down for the sake of his family. The family comes first in all of the decisions that he makes.

When a true father makes a decision, he makes it on the basis of what is in the best interest of his children. It is very easy to receive fathering from this type of a person. It is easy to listen to someone that you know cares about you.

3. *A HEART OF PATIENCE:* Parenting requires a lot of patience because children make a lot of mistakes. They make a lot of mistakes because they are children who lack experience. Apostolic ministries are constantly working with people and leaders who lack experience or have a limited frame of reference.

If apostolic ministries are to be effective with the spiritual children that God has placed in their charge, they must possess great patience (see 2 Corinthians 12:12). They will often times be ministering to the immature—those who have found themselves in trouble and need adjustment or correction.

4. *A HEART OF FAITHFULNESS:* A father's heart is a faithful heart. A father's relationship to his children is not a fair weather relationship. Jesus said, *"I will never leave you nor forsake you"* (Hebrews 13:5). Even if you don't do everything right all of the time, God will be with you. Even if you forsake him, He will not forsake you.

Loyalty to people and the local church are crucial if the apostle is to enjoy a lifetime of pleasant fruit.

Unfortunately many ministries, like many natural fathers, are not able to remain constant when relationships are tested. That results in a life of broken and unfulfilled relationships.

The Apostle as a Father

Using Paul as our example again, we see that even though Paul had no natural children, he had abundant opportunity to express his father's heart and raise up a spiritual heritage in the Lord. Paul not only saw himself as a father, he also had the spiritual fruit of a father. His fruit as a father fell into four different categories:

1. *FATHERING BELIEVERS.* First of all, Paul fathered believers. As a church planting apostle, Paul's first order of business in any community was to win individuals to Christ. If he was to plant a church, he had to begin one person at a time. Paul had an evangelist's heart that was manifested by a great love for lost people.

   Every apostle must share this passion. The heart of the father in the apostle reaches down to the smallest level—that of the individual. An apostolic heart is not just concerned with crowds, but beats deeply for every person with whom it comes into contact.

   Even when Paul was under house arrest in Rome, he was still birthing new babies into the kingdom of God. He was even concerned about a seemingly insignificant runaway slave that he met by the name of Onesimus (see Philemon 10). Even when he might have focused only on the difficulty of his personal situation, Paul was still sharing his faith and bearing spiritual offspring.

2. *FATHERING MINISTRIES.* The second way to examine the father heart of Paul is through his relation to other ministries. Paul was a spiritual father to many young, developing ministries. It appears that the call to apostolic ministry involves an anointing to raise up and release others into ministry.

Not every pastor or leader seems to have this anointing. Paul definitely had it. Wherever he went, it seems that someone was with him being trained to do what he was doing. Timothy was one of those that traveled with Paul. We know Paul fathered his ministry as Paul referred to Timothy as his son in the Gospel (see Philippians 2:22; 1 Corinthians 4:17). He had many other spiritual sons who were able to carry on his work after he departed.

Some have said that there is no success without a successor. For the apostolic church planter, this is always true. When Paul established churches, he had to be able to disciple ministries and raise up leaders. Because he was only able to stay in a given place for a short time, he had to be able to reproduce his leadership in others rather quickly.

3. *FATHERING CHURCHES.* The third way in which Paul's heart was displayed is through his fathering of local churches. Paul referred to the Corinthian church as the seal, or proof, of his apostleship (see 1 Corinthians 9:2). Wherever Paul went, churches sprang up.

The fostering of church plants and the nurturing of churches will mark all apostolic ministry. This does not necessarily mean that every apostle will plant a string of churches themselves, but the fruit of their ministry will be the existence of local churches.

I have known many ministries that I would call apostolic but have planted only one church. However, many churches have been in the heart of that ministry. They planted an apostolic church where they focused on training leaders that would be sent forth to plant other churches. They trained leaders, equipped them, sent them, encouraged them, and followed up on them. The new local churches that have resulted were just as much their offspring as any they would have started themselves.

4. *FATHERING OTHER APOSTOLIC MINISTRIES.* There is a biblical principle of reproduction that goes all the way back to the first chapter of Genesis. The statement "like begets like" would be a good paraphrase of this principle. True ministries bring forth after their kind (see Genesis 1:11-12).

One of the marks of a true apostolic ministry is that apostles are able to reproduce other apostolic ministries. Teachers will reproduce teachers, evangelists will reproduce evangelists, prophets will reproduce prophets, pastors will reproduce pastors, and apostles will reproduce apostles.

This is illustrated in Acts 11 and 13. Paul, who was a teacher at the time, and Barnabas, who had more of a prophetic ministry, labored in Antioch for a couple of years bringing order to the wave of new converts. The result of their efforts is seen in Acts 13:1, where after two or more years, the church in Antioch was characterized by the existence of *"certain prophets and teachers."* Paul and Barnabas had successfully reproduced themselves in others.

In the same way, apostolic ministries should have the ability to reproduce that same ministry in others. Paul, again, is the classic example of this. Most of the post-ascension apostles that are named in the New Testament were in some way discipled by, or connected to, Paul (i.e. Timothy, Silas, Titus, Epaphras, etc.). When Paul left this life as a martyr, his work went on through others.

The Work of the Apostle

As you study the life and ministry of those named apostles in the New Testament, it becomes very apparent that no two apostles were exactly alike in their work and ministry. This is just like God. Even though we have general categories of ministry, every person is quite different in their expression of personality and function in that ministry.

Because of this, it is essential not to become too stereotypical in our discussion of any ministry. If we were to make all prophets fit into one mold, we would lose something of the manifold glory of God that is seen in the diversity. The same is true in apostolic ministry. We would do God an injustice if we were too limiting and restrictive in our definitions.

In spite of this, however, there are some common threads that seem to run through the Scripture when attempting to piece together a profile of this ministry. The work of an apostle includes, but is not limited to, the following:

1. *APOSTOLIC MINISTRIES WILL BE ZEALOUS TO ESTABLISH AND PRESERVE APOSTOLIC DOCTRINE.* One of the things that was important to the twelve apostles of the Lamb, and is also clearly evident in the life and ministry of the apostle Paul, was a solid doctrinal foundation for the church. The Twelve spent much of their initial ministry making sure that the Jerusalem church, which was the first church, was built on a solid doctrinal foundation (see Acts 2:42).

Paul and Barnabas shared this concern as they laid the foundation for the church in Antioch. They were thrilled with the wave of evangelism that was taking place in the area, but they also knew that if this local church were to become a mighty army for the Lord, it would have to be grounded in the truth. For this reason, they spent at least two years indoctrinating the church (see Acts 11:26).

As you read Paul's letters, especially to Timothy, you sense Paul's passion for truth and pure doctrine. Paul challenged Timothy to continually give himself to the Word of God. Paul realized that the foundation of the house is the most important part in determining the strength and destiny of that house.

Apostolic ministry would not by its very nature be driven by the new, the novel, the experiential, or the subjective. Apostolic ministry would be concerned that the basis for what is done is firmly rooted in the clearly revealed and rightly divided Word of God (see Acts 15:1-31).

2. *APOSTOLIC MINISTRIES WILL BE INVOLVED IN FOUNDING AND ESTABLISHING LOCAL CHURCHES ON A PROPER FOUNDATION.* When Paul wrote about apostles and prophets he refers to them as foundation ministries (see Ephesians 2:20; 3:5). Whether he is referring to the twelve apostles or the post-ascension apostles, it is clear that apostles are connected to the word "foundation."

It is interesting that when Paul went to Ephesus he found some disciples. He could have started building his church right then. Instead, he gave these disciples a little quiz to find out what their experience had been to that point. As he quizzed them, he realized they did not have a complete experience. Before he would build on this foundation, he made sure that all of these disciples were on the same page.

Paul did not take anything for granted when it came to building the church—it was serious business as far as he was concerned. So before he began working with these disciples, he took them back to the issues of repentance, faith, water baptism, and the baptism of the Holy Spirit (see Acts 19:1-7).

Paul understood that he was a foundation ministry. As such, he was always concerned about foundation issues. Paul was a sort of spiritual foundation inspector. He laid the foundation of one church after another and was concerned that whoever built on his foundation did it with the same care that he had used when he laid the foundation (see 1 Corinthians 3:10).

This burden of Paul was seen in several ways. It was seen in his concern that new converts had a proper start (see Philemon 10). It was seen in his concern that believers not stray from their foundation in Christ (see Colossians 2:6-7). It was seen in his concern that young ministers not neglect the basics and the Word in their ministries (see 2 Timothy 2:14-19). It was seen in his concern for the churches that he had personally established (see Galatians 1:6-7) and it was seen in his burden for all of the churches (see 2 Corinthians 11:28).

3. *APOSTOLIC MINISTRIES WILL BE INVOLVED IN THE FEEDING, TRAINING, AND RELEASING OF OTHER MINISTRIES.* As was indicated earlier, it seems apparent that one of the marks of an apostolic ministry is the grace to raise up and release other ministries. This is a grace that should not be taken for granted. Not all pastors and church leaders are able to do this.

Along with this grace comes the ability to recognize the potential in emerging ministries, patience to help these ministries through their formative years, ability to mentor and equip these ministries into a place of usefulness, and a commitment to see them reach their own place of fruitfulness.

I greatly appreciate a man that I have known for many years who was not afraid to identify his ministry as that of an apostle when it was risky to do so. One of the qualities that I saw in him, and can also be seen in Paul, was his relationship to young ministries. He never did anything alone. Not that he needed a lot of help. But he always had a young person, or minister in training, along with him watching, learning, and functioning at their level.

Some have referred to an apostle as *a pastor of pastors*. This is a good description. It does not mean that the apostle will only minister to other ministers. It means, however, that the apostle has a special eye, burden, and heart for those called to leadership in the body of Christ. Pastors cry too. Pastors need pastoring too.

Church leaders cannot readily go to their congregations for counsel and spiritual support. It is good for them to be able to look to fathering ministries in the body of Christ for pastoral care.

4. *APOSTOLIC MINISTRIES WILL BE INVOLVED IN FOLLOWING UP ON THE CHURCHES AND LEADERS FOR WHICH THEY ARE RESPONSIBLE THROUGH CARE, ENCOURAGEMENT, AND CORRECTION AS NEEDED.* A good deal of Paul's time was spent in follow-up ministry to the churches that he and others had founded. Paul did not start churches or raise up ministries and then leave them on their own. In fact, Paul's second missionary journey began with a conversation with Barnabas that went something like this, "Hey Barney, let's go back and see if those churches we began earlier are still doing all right" (see Acts 15:36).

Not only did Paul follow up through visits, he followed up by sending others to visit and exchanging letters with those churches and their leaders. We have been blessed by much of Paul's follow-up mail. On those visits and in those letters, Paul often had to get involved in some of the specific problems that were being faced by the churches and their leaders.

As fathering ministries, apostles are not involved with the churches to win popularity contests, increase their mailing list, or receive financial support; they are involved with a goal to serve, assist, and strengthen both the leadership and the churches. They are involved to contribute their part to the overall success of each local church.

In this sense, an apostle is *a trouble-shooting ministry.* True apostolic ministries are willing to get their hands dirty with the problems of other leaders and churches.

5. *APOSTOLIC MINISTRIES WILL BE A RESOURCE TO OTHER LOCAL CHURCHES AND THEIR LEADERS AS THE NEED ARISES.* Because Paul had such a strong father's heart and love for the churches, he made himself available to other churches and their leadership teams. Even when Paul was in prison in Rome, he was willing to get involved with a man by the name of Epaphras and some problems that were happening at his church in Colossae (see Colossians 1:7; 4:2).

Paul had not founded the church in Colossae, but because he had a big heart that did not just include his own vineyard, he was called upon by others as a resource. Many ministries only work with their piece of the pie. If it does not personally relate to them, they are not available for help. Apostolic ministries are able to see and literally carry a burden for the needs of other leaders and churches in the body of Christ.

Many apostolic leaders end up reaching out to other pastors and leaders in their geographical region. They love to bring leaders together for fellowship, mutual edification, equipping, and mission fulfillment. They may even find themselves organizing minister's fellowships that are designed to strengthen, equip, and envision like-minded leaders. These leaders and their churches actually become their spiritual congregation.

Ministry After Ones Heart

Apostolic ministry is not something that you can manufacture. It must come from the heart. It cannot come out of the heart unless it is in the heart. Apostolic ministry must first and foremost be a heart ministry.

Every ministry that a person has will be a reflection of what is in the heart. Whatever you have at heart will end up being the object of your ministry. If you love the kingdom of God, you will love the instrument of God, the church. If you have a heart and burden for leaders in the church and the ability to minister to their needs, God will give you a ministry whereby you can minister to these needs.

God wants to give all of us a ministry that is after our heart. Such ministry will not be drudgery. We will have the grace, faith, and gifting that we need to fulfill all of His perfect will for our lives.

Apostolic ministry is a function, not a title. There is a work that Christ wants to accomplish and He has called individuals in His body to be His extended hands in that area. Christ wants fathering ministries or servants who reflect His heart of love for the people and purposes of God. The need is great, not for people with more titles, but for people who will lay their lives down for others.

8

APOSTOLIC PREPARATION

"And I thank Christ Jesus our Lord who has enabled me, because He counted me faithful, putting me into the ministry." (1 TIMOTHY 1:12)

If God has called you to be an apostle, how do you get ready? There are very few schools that offer a major in apostolic ministry. There are no places from which you can purchase a starter kit that will set you up in apostolic ministry. Yet we have to believe that there are many in the body of Christ today who have an apostolic call on their life.

I do not believe that apostolic ministry is meant to be a rare expression in the body of Christ—reserved only for select company. If the New Testament is to be the pattern for ministry in the world today (and I believe it is), it would be easy to conclude that apostolic ministry will abound.

When it comes to a study of the five-fold ministry in the New Testament, prophets are mentioned a few times, the evangelist is specifically mentioned a couple of times, pastors and teachers are referred to occasionally, but apostles are mentioned often.

We have to conclude that God's desire is that many find their way into this ministry of an apostle. Because there is a great need for new churches, there is a need for those who can father ministries in the body of Christ. The church needs those who can serve as a fatherly resource to pastors and their churches. But how does that happen? How does one become an apostle?

Becoming an apostle has a lot in common with becoming any ministry in the body of Christ. It is similar to going to college to train for a specialized career. Before you get real specific in your training, you have to take the general courses that serve as a foundation to all occupations. At this stage, your training to be an engineer does not look that much different from another person's training to be a doctor. There are certain basic skills or courses of study that are foundational to both.

It does not really matter if God has called you to be an apostle, a prophet, an evangelist, a pastor, or a teacher. Everyone must begin his or her preparation the same way. The foundation for all ministries is the same.

Being a Christian

It begins with being a Christian who is fully submitted to the Lordship of Christ in all areas. This includes a strong personal relationship with the Lord that is characterized by a life of prayer and daily meditation in the Word of God. Many people want to talk about their future destiny but seem unmotivated to lay the simplest foundations for their future.

The foundation for apostolic ministry is the same as the foundation for our Christian lives. Our foundation is a lifestyle of hearing and responding to the voice of the Holy Spirit every day. The fruit of this kind of lifestyle will be apparent to all. People who live this kind of life do well on their jobs, have exemplary marriages, enjoy families that are a model for others to follow, and have lives that are characterized by dedication, loyalty, the fruit of the Spirit, and righteousness, peace and joy in the Holy Ghost.

Becoming Faithful

When Paul talked of his own choosing by God, he indicated that it was his faithfulness that caught God's eye (see 1 Timothy 1:12). God saw in Paul a man who had been faithful, was currently faithful, and in all likelihood would continue to be faithful long into the future. So many young ministries want to sidestep this aspect of their development. Jesus, however, made it clear that the road to maturity would be marked by three tests of faithfulness (see Luke 16:10-12).

The first test of faithfulness is learning to be faithful in that which is least (see Luke 16:10), or as Matthew says, *"faithful over a few things"* (25:21). Many want to start at the top. They want to have authority over things of consequence. How arrogant it is of us to believe that God is going to entrust His most precious possessions (i.e. His people) to us when we have not proven ourselves with things that are small and of little value. God knows that we cannot be trusted with many things or much until we have demonstrated a spirit of faithfulness in all areas. This means being willing to be faithful *before* we have ministry responsibility.

The second test of faithfulness is learning to be faithful with natural riches, or money (see Luke 16:11). Paul had certainly proven his faithfulness in the area of his money. He had learned how to work hard with his hands. He had saved his own money for his future ministry. He worked hard to support himself and others in his eventual ministry.

Paul did not learn these things after he was released into apostolic ministry, he learned these things first. He was faithful first and then God released him to function in his calling. God could trust Paul with true, spiritual riches because Paul was faithful with natural riches.

The third test of faithfulness is learning to be faithful with that which belongs to another man (see Luke 16:12). Can you be faithful in your own local assembly to serve the senior leadership that has been placed over you in the Lord and in effect serve another man's vision? Can you become a strong, contributing member of a local church even when all of your efforts are going to bless the ministry of another? Jesus said that we should not expect to be given what is our own if we do not have the ability to be faithful where we have been planted. It is simple. People should not be given authority if they have not demonstrated an ability in their personal life to submit to authority and serve with gladness.

Becoming a Servant

After Paul got saved, he wanted to start his ministry right away (see Acts 9:20). He tried to go into Jerusalem and preach, but he did not get the response that he was after. In fact, no one believed that he was converted and they did not want anything to do with him (see Acts 9:26). The truth is, Paul was not a ready instrument in the hands of the Lord.

Paul had a lot of dying to do. He had to die to himself, his own plans, his former concepts of ministry, and his future aspirations. A careful study of the life of Paul indicates that this man had great ambitions. Prior to his conversion, he was training to be a leader in his nation. He also seems to have been prone to boasting in his own accomplishments and abilities.

This all would have to change if God was going to use him. Paul was not afforded the opportunity to sit at the feet of Jesus. He had not heard Jesus' teaching on the key to greatness. He was still functioning with a worldly mentality of pushing and clawing his way to the top. He had not heard Jesus say, *"whoever of you desires to be first shall be slave of all."* (Mark 10:44).

Because of this, Paul had to go through his emptying process. Much like Moses in the Old Testament, Paul had to go through his wilderness experience and be emptied of self and personal ambition. God wanted to get Paul into a place of dependency. He wanted Paul to learn how to serve others.

This process is different for every person. For Paul, it seems to have taken from ten to thirteen years in Arabia and Tarsus.

For Moses it took a little longer—forty years! But when the preparation was complete and all of the self-confidence had been extracted, the vessel was ready for the master's use.

Paul seems to have understood this process. He would train others to enter into apostolic ministry and function, but he would make sure at the same time that they had their opportunity to learn to be a servant first and a leader second.

This is why Paul took Timothy, John Mark, Titus, and others on his journeys with him (see Acts 13:5). They would be exposed to apostolic ministry, but more than that they would have an opportunity to serve. Paul had seen many self-serving ministries (see Philippians 1:15-16; 1 Thessalonians 2:1-6). He had no desire to see any more of them.

Qualifying as an Elder

Once you are a faithful, serving Christian, you can begin to think about leadership in the church. While not every leader will be an elder of a local church in the strict sense, every leader should aspire to meet the qualifications listed for those who desire to be an elder. When Paul listed these qualifications, I do not think he was setting up a higher standard of Christianity. I believe that these qualities were simply meant to reflect what a good Christian was to look like.

Someone who wants to be used in any leadership capacity must be a model believer that others can follow. In fact, people are instructed in the Bible to follow the lifestyle of their leaders (see Hebrews 13:7). That means that if God has called you to be an apostle, you need to aspire to qualify yourself in the areas that will establish you as a leader in other people's eyes. That means that the aspiring leader should study 1 Timothy 3 and Titus 1 where Paul lists leadership qualifications.

Aspiring to ministry then becomes aspiring to see these qualities worked in your life before being sent forth. This means you need to focus on several areas of development as you prepare for the call of God on your life. Deficiency in any one of these areas could have a profound effect on the success of your ministry.

1. *CHARACTER DEVELOPMENT:* Many of the qualities on Paul's list deal with the personal character of the potential leader. Paul could have listed all of the fruit of the Spirit I am sure, but he focused on character issues such as temperance, self-control, holiness, and patience.

   All of these qualities are essential if you are going to be able to act as a spiritual father to converts, leaders, and churches. You must be emptied of selfishness and your own personal agenda if you are going to have what it takes to bring baby Christians to maturity.

2. *PEOPLE SKILLS:* Apostolic ministry is a people-orientated ministry. An apostle cannot be hard, harsh, angry, violent, or unapproachable. The apostle must have the heart of a pastor who genuinely cares about the needs of the sheep.

   The apostle must have the ability to function with a spirit of gentleness, as he may often be called upon to arbitrate in delicate situations. If an apostle is quick-tempered, he can easily become part of the problem rather than part of the solution.

   Paul's heart for people was reflected in the letters that he wrote to the churches he founded. To the Thessalonians he wrote, *"we were gentle among you, just as a nursing mother cherishes her own children. So, affectionately longing for you, we were well pleased to impart to you not only the gospel of God, but also our own lives, because you had become dear to us"* (1 Thessalonians 2:7-8). To the Philippians he wrote, *"I have you in my heart"*

(Philippians 1:7) and *"I long for you with all the affection of Jesus Christ"* (Philippians 1:8).

3. *FAMILY RELATIONSHIPS:* Not every apostle will necessarily have a family. Paul, we know, was not married and did not have any natural children. However, he was an exception, even in his day (see 1 Corinthians 9:5). Most apostolic ministries will be married and will most likely have children from that marriage.

   The family of the leader constitutes the leader's first church. In the family there is the leadership team of husband and wife and they have the congregation in their children. In this sense, the home becomes the proving ground for all ministry.

   I do not mean that anyone should ever look at the home as a stepping stone to his or her ministry. However, the home is a place where the principles and practices of a person are manifest without hypocrisy. It becomes the place where one's true ministry becomes evident.

   It takes the same kind of leadership to raise up a good family that it takes to raise up a good church. The home is really a miniature church. It is a place of prayer, worship, fellowship, and communion with the Lord.

   Paul said that no one should serve as a leader in the church unless they had done well as a leader in their home. They should have an exemplary marriage and children who honor God in their testimony.

4. *FINANCIAL STABILITY:* There is no place for greed in the work of the Lord. Money can be a great stumbling block in the ministry. Paul said that if you are going to be a leader, you need to deal with the issue of money.

   Apostolic ministries will have the power to abuse in this area. Paul was very careful with money. He went overboard to eliminate suspicion—to the point that he personally financed his entire enterprise (until he was arrested and could not work). Sometimes he did not accept support that was rightfully his in order to avoid reproach in this area.

God wants us to deal with our attitude toward money early on in our preparation experience. He wants us to know how to work, how to get our hands dirty, how to live within our means, and how to be responsible for ourselves and for others. This is why having our finances in order is such an important foundation for ministry.

5. *DOCTRINAL PURITY:* Paul makes it very clear that all those who want to be in leadership must be students of the Word of God. Our ministry is dependent on our ability to rightly divide the Word of Truth. It does not matter if you are called to be an apostle, a prophet, an evangelist, a pastor, or a teacher. All of these ministries must operate in a symbiotic relationship with the Word of God.

That means study and preparation. That means making some sacrifices to attend Bible school or some other training program. That means setting aside other pursuits and running after the call of God when there are so many other distractions.

The only way to come to a place where you can hold the mystery of the faith in a pure conscience (see 1 Timothy 3:9), exhort and convict with sound doctrine (see Titus 1:9), and hold fast the faithful word (see Titus 1:9), is to give yourself to the Word of God in an ongoing way. It is then that you can become a worker who does not need to be ashamed (see 2 Timothy 2:15).

The early church was nurtured by the Apostles' doctrine. The early apostles had to fight to maintain their time in the Word (see Acts 6:1-6). However, if modern-day apostles are going to keep the church in a place of balance as winds of doctrine blow across the land, apostolic ministries must be steeped in the Word.

6. *LIFE TESTIMONY:* The future apostle must learn to live like an apostle in the present. You do not have to wait to be sent out to be an apostle. You can begin right now in your family. You can begin right now on your job. You can begin right now in your neighborhood. Reach out to people now! Disciple new converts right now! Teach and train people in the right ways of God right now! Become a father to the fatherless right now!

   Many people are looking so far into the future for God to do something through their life that they fail to see the opportunities right in front of them. If you desire to be a leader, your preparation process will continue until you can maintain a good testimony among both the saved and the unsaved, among both those inside of the church and those outside of the church (see 1 Timothy 3:7).

Proving Yourself at Home

Where does apostolic ministry begin? It begins at home. It begins in the local church. Paul did not go from obscurity to his apostolic function. When Barnabas sent for Saul, he brought him to Antioch where Saul became a functioning member of the congregation.

He came under the leadership of Barnabas, a man who had been in leadership in Jerusalem prior to being sent to Antioch. He came under the leadership of a man he would eventually exceed in ministry function.

Paul did not begin as an apostle. He began his official ministry as an assistant and a teacher. He worked with new converts, helping to lay foundations in their lives and be transformed into model Christians (see Acts 11:26).

As Paul did everything he could to make Barnabas, the church of Antioch, and the new converts a success, his gifts made room for him. He excelled to the point that everyone in his local assembly recognized his calling.

Paul did not have to push his way out the door and into apostolic function. He was faithful in his first calling as a teacher. Paul was faithful to those over him in the Lord, and he was faithful to the local church where God had placed him. Because of that, God opened the door of greater influence to Paul—to assist Barnabas on a missionary journey and do in other places what they had done in Antioch.

Paul's gift made room for him on the local level. As Paul taught and ministered in Antioch, people's lives were changed. As he discipled new converts, people became more Christlike. As he was faithful to fulfill his call, he was able to raise up and release other teaching ministries.

Paul had been asked to help in a situation that needed teachers. He spent a couple of years ministering. When he was done with that assignment, teachers were functioning in Antioch (see Acts 13:1).

Paul had effectively demonstrated at home what he wanted to do on the field. He had demonstrated his ability to father new converts. He had demonstrated his ability to bring these converts to maturity. He had demonstrated an ability to equip and release ministry in others. He had demonstrated his ability to establish a strong, reproducing local church.

There are many young ministries today that are looking to be sent out into the field without a clear demonstration of proving themselves at home. If local elders and deacons need to be proven first (see 1 Timothy 3:6,10), why would it be any less for those who are sent out into apostolic church planting?

I remember talking to a young man who had a desire to be sent to the mission field to establish a church. I was not surprised by his request because he had been raised in the country to which he desired to be sent. The problem was, as his pastor, I did not see this kind of fruit in his life in our local church.

I remember asking him what he would do if we sent him out. "How would you begin?" I asked him. He told me that he would teach English and use that as a means to bring people to Christ and gather converts for the foundation of the church.

I think my next questions surprised him. I asked, "How many people have you brought to the Lord in the last five years in this church? How many people are in our church today by your efforts alone?" Unfortunately the answer was "None."

I continued, "Do you think it's easier to bring someone to Christ in another culture or your own culture? Do you think it's easier to talk to people about Christ where there is no culture and language barrier than where there is a huge culture and language barrier?"

Somehow this young man had the idea that he would become his desired ministry when he reached the field. No! The place to become what you want to be is right in the greenhouse of the local church, under the tutelage of pastors and leaders who can assist you in your growth and development.

I appreciated this young man's passion, but he was not being very realistic. He wanted the elders of the church to lay hands on him and send him out when he had not demonstrated to anyone that he could do what he said he felt called to do. Paul had the fruit of ministry *before* he was sent out to function fully in his calling.

I challenged this young man to become in the local church what he wanted to be on the field. I encouraged him to reach out in a new way to the unsaved right around him. I told him that in the next couple of years, if he could point me to five families in the church who were serving God and in the church by his efforts alone, I would be the first one to lay my hands on his head and send him to the land of his calling.

Mentoring

A key part of the preparation process for any ministry is that of being mentored by older, more experienced ministries of the same order. There is no question that teachers have the ability to reproduce teachers, prophets release prophets and so on. Apostolic ministries should also give birth to other apostolic ministries.

Barnabas and Paul began their association with a mentoring relationship. Barnabas was a leader from the Jerusalem church who seemed to have a heart for ministries who were struggling to become what God had called them to be. He reached out to Saul when no one else wanted anything to do with him (see Acts 9:27). Later he did the same thing to John Mark, a man even Paul had given up on (see Acts 15:37-39). That is why the apostles named him Barnabas, which means "son of encouragement" (see Acts 4:36).

Barnabas had the heart of a father and was willing to invest himself into those younger ministries who had a call but needed some fine tuning if they were going to be productive in that call. Barnabas' first project was Saul. When Barnabas came to Antioch, he sent to Tarsus for Saul and had him work with him to lay the foundation of the Antioch church (see Acts 11:25).

We will talk more about mentoring in the next chapter, but for our purposes now, I will say that for mentoring to take place, senior ministries must be willing to get a genuine burden for younger ministries. It also takes younger ministries who are willing to submit to older ministries they may one day supersede.

To summarize this area of preparation, I would like to quote from my book, *The New Testament Church and Its Ministries* (page 90):

> "When you put all of these things together you find some keys that apply to practically all who would be used in this ministry.

1. The apostle will have a definite call of God to this ministry.

2. The apostle will have to have a thorough knowledge of the Scripture.

3. The apostle will experience a period of preparation covering several years during which he will prove himself and his ministry on the local level by which he will gain the necessary wisdom, knowledge and experience.

4. The apostle will usually train specifically for a time under the ministry of other apostles.

5. The apostle will not be sent by God until the preparation is complete.

6. The call and timing of the going of the apostle will be confirmed by the brethren among whom he is ministering.

7. The sending church will participate and identify with the work of the apostle by the laying on of hands (see Acts 13:1-3).

8. The apostle goes forth in the power of the Spirit, often times in company with others, to do the work God has called him [or her] to do."

9

APOSTOLIC MENTORING

"But I trust in the Lord Jesus to send Timothy to you shortly, that I may also be encouraged when I know your state. For I have no one like-minded, who will sincerely care for your state. For all seek their own, not the things which are of Christ Jesus."

(PHILIPPIANS 2:20-21)

What a wonderful thing it must have been for Paul to have a spiritual son like Timothy! What a wonderful thing it must have been for Timothy to have a spiritual father like Paul! Both were able to assist each other through the mentoring process.

From Paul's perspective, it was great to have a younger ministry who was full of strength that could be relied upon. Paul was under house arrest in Rome and yet still had a desire to follow up on the churches that he had established. How could he know how the churches were doing if he could not personally visit them? The answer, he could send Timothy.

Timothy was a man Paul knew could be trusted. He was a man he knew would faithfully evaluate the situation. A man who would handle any problem the same way he would. A man of proven character that would genuinely care for the sheep and would give himself to Paul's fruit the same way Paul would have.

Timothy was Paul's son in the faith who had undoubtedly come to Christ on Paul's first visit to Lystra. Timothy had seen both the high points and the low points of apostolic ministry. He had witnessed the high points when Paul spoke the word of healing to the lame man and saw him rise and walk (see Acts 14:8-10). He had seen how the people of his region wanted to exalt this apostolic ministry and reverence it as a god (see Acts 14:11-13).

However, he also witnessed the low points of ministry and the fickleness of the crowd who one moment were proclaiming the apostles as gods and the next moment were taking up stones to kill them (see Acts 14:19-20). Perhaps he was among those who had to pray for Paul's life to return to him after the stoning.

Who could have known at this point that Timothy himself would be an apostolic ministry (see 1 Thessalonians 1:1; 2:6)? Who could have known at this point that Paul and Timothy would become a model for ministry development and relationship? Who could have known that leaders for years to come would speak of "Timothys" as a way of referring to leadership trainees?

Leaders are Made, not Born

There is no question that there are a lot of potential Timothys out there. There are many people who have a strong call of God on their lives. There are many individuals that God would seek to use in apostolic ministry in our day.

But these leaders do not come fully trained and ready to be sent forth. More often than not, these potential leaders are plagued by negative attitudes and other imperfections that would hinder them from becoming all God desires for them to become.

These young leaders need spiritual fathers; they need mentors who can take time with them and help them shape their lives into an arrow that can be shot forth to hit the target (see Isaiah 49:1-2). Just as natural fathers need to shape the arrows (natural children) that God places in their hands (see Psalm 127:4), God is looking for spiritual fathers to shape spiritual sons and daughters into effective instruments of the Lord.

Paul may not have had any natural children, but God gave him many spiritual offspring. Paul understood that children do not raise themselves. That is why God gave them parents who, hopefully, are older and wiser, and can guide them on the way. Spiritual children also have a difficult time raising themselves. They need senior ministries to lead and guide them into productivity. This is not to say that every ministry has had the advantage of such mentoring. Some have had to come up the hard way. However, it is much better when true spiritual fathers take initiative in this area of developing and equipping the ministries of the future.

Leaders Must be Discipled

Jesus, Barnabas, and Paul all serve as wonderful examples of this father's heart. Jesus, as the apostle of heaven, was sent by the Father to build His church. Jesus was interested in laying the foundation on which all other churches would be built. His first order of business in this process was to mentor twelve other ministries in the apostolic function.

Barnabas was sent by the Jerusalem church to help establish the Antioch church. However, it is clear that Barnabas had a vision that was much greater than Antioch. He had a vision for the world. The only way he would be able to contribute in a significant way to this world vision was to become a mentor of ministries that could take his place in leadership in Antioch and also be sent out to assist in his work overseas. He mentored Paul. He also mentored John Mark, who went on to author the Gospel that bears his name.

Paul followed the model of Barnabas. Paul began as the pupil of Barnabas (see Acts 13:2,7). He soon became the leader of their team (see Acts 13:13) and eventually a leader of an apostolic team of his own (see Acts 15:40). When he set out with his own team, being paired with Silas, he chose Timothy to travel with them as his servant and pupil (see Acts 16:1-3). (It should be noted that before Timothy accompanied Paul in this capacity, he had already proven himself at home and was *"well spoken of by the brethren"* in his own local church [Acts 16:2].)

Mentoring is a lot like apprenticeship. An apprentice is someone who is linked with an experienced artisan. An apprentice learns the tricks of the trade by watching, assisting, and eventually doing, all under the watchful eye of the master. Hopefully, the apprentice can learn a lot from the experience of the past so that he will not have to learn everything by trial and error.

If we use Jesus as our pattern, we see that mentoring involves at least seven things:

1. *SPENDING TIME WITH THE APPRENTICE.* When Jesus chose His disciples after an all-night prayer meeting (see Luke 6:12-16), He chose them first and foremost *"that He might be with them"* (Mark. 3:14). Other translations of this passage state that he chose them *"as His companions"* (NEB) or *"to associate with Him"* (Rieu). Jesus was going to spend time with them and let them accompany him on His journeys.

   I have always appreciated ministries who have made it possible for younger ministries to travel with them. I remember one of the first men I knew that exemplified apostolic ministry. I noticed that he would always be accompanied in his travels by one of his Timothys.

   This is not an easy thing to do. It is difficult to give up a certain amount of privacy and independence, but ministries who will in fact mentor other ministries will have to be willing to include others in what they do.

   Younger ministries will learn a great deal by just watching the life and ministry of their mentor. The disciples learned a great deal about ministering by simply watching the Master in action. I am amazed as I read the account of Peter raising Tabitha from the dead (see Acts 9:36-41) to see how closely it resembles what Jesus did when he raised a girl from the dead (see Mark 5:35-43). Step by step, Peter did exactly what he had seen Jesus do.

   There is no question that we learn best by example. Many people could never learn how to use a computer if it came down to their being able to read and understand the manuals that accompany them. However, if you can just get someone who understands them to spend a little time with you and show you a few things, you can learn very quickly.

So many Scriptures emphasize the power of the leader's example. We teach more by what we do than by what we say. Leaders must be willing to let their light shine before the people they hope to train. Their light is their life (see John 1:4).

Paul did not model the kind of leadership that separates itself. He did not model what is at times referred to as "ministerial aloofness." He followed the example of Jesus and was willing to bring others into his every day experience.

Notice Paul's statements that reflect this posture on his part:

"Therefore I urge you, imitate me." (1 CORINTHIANS 4:16)

"Imitate me, just as I also imitate Christ." (1 CORINTHIANS 11:1)

"Brethren, join in following my example, and note those who so walk, as you have us for a pattern." (PHILIPPIANS 3:17)

"And you became followers of us and of the Lord, having received the word in much affliction, with joy of the Holy Spirit, so that you became examples to all in Macedonia and Achaia who believe." (1 THESSALONIANS 1:6-7)

"For you yourselves know how you ought to follow us, for we were not disorderly among you; nor did we eat anyone's bread free of charge, but worked with labor and toil night and day, that we might not be a burden to any of you, not because we do not have authority, but to make ourselves an example of how you should follow us."
(2 THESSALONIANS 3:7-9)

"However, for this reason I obtained mercy, that in me first Jesus Christ might show all longsuffering, as a pattern to those who are going to believe on Him for everlasting life." (TIMOTHY 1:16)

One of the greatest things that Jesus gave to us was His example. We are saved from our sins by His death. But we are also saved by His life in that He was the Word made flesh (see John 1:14). When we see what He did, we can answer the question, "How shall we then live?" As with so many young people today we can ask, "What Would Jesus Do?"

If a leader is going to let his or her example be the teacher, then the leader must be willing to be that example. The leader cannot have the Charles Barkley mentality, "I am not a role model." The leader must be willing to teach by example on the job and at play.

2. *PRAYING FOR THE APPRENTICE.* One of the things that both Jesus and Paul did was pray regularly for those under their charge. Jesus even told Peter that He had prayed for him that his faith would not fail (see Luke 22:32). Paul spent much time in prayer for those who looked to him for leadership as well. Paul opens almost every one of his letters by indicating the substance of those prayers.

If you want to develop a strong burden for people, spend quality time in prayer for them. Not only will God increase your burden for them, but He will also give you significant insight into their life. This information from the Spirit will be highly beneficial as you seek to mentor them into a place of leadership.

Praying for them should include three aspects of prayer. First, it should involve regular daily prayer for them in the privacy of your prayer closet. Jesus seems to have done this on the many occasions He withdrew Himself to pray (see Luke 22:32).

Second, it should involve praying with them one on one or as a group. Jesus used this method both to bless His followers but also to teach them how to pray. He was a model for them who taught by example in this important area.

Third, it should involve praying for them with the laying on of hands. Paul speaks of praying prayers of impartation for his son Timothy (see 1 Timothy 4:14; 2 Timothy 1:6). Often, as you pray over Timothy ministries there is a communication and impartation of your faith and vision to them. At the same time, those ministries receive encouragement to allow God to work His purposes deep within their spirit.

3. *SYSTEMATIC INSTRUCTION.* Even though there is a focus on relationship in the mentoring process, it is critical that systematic instruction be an important element in the process. Jesus spent a great deal of His time in systematic instruction, and even more time assisting His disciples in understanding exactly what He was saying (see Matthew 5:1-7:29; 13:3-52).

Jesus made it clear that making disciples included *"teaching them to observe all things"* (Matthew 28:20).

Unfortunately, there is a real lack today in teaching to equip ministries. As a result, there are many apostles building on a faulty foundation.

When Paul tutored Timothy, he focused on five areas. First, he focused on the Bible (see 2 Timothy 3:15-17). In that passage, Paul made it clear that knowledge of the Scriptures will not only make you wise unto salvation, but it will also help you become *"thoroughly equipped for every good work."* Apostolic ministries need to give themselves to the Word of God and prayer (see Acts 6:4). The Word of God is the main tool in their hands to accomplish their ministry.

Second, Paul focused on doctrine (see 1 Timothy 4:6; 2 Timothy 3:10; Titus 1:9; 2:1). Paul wanted to be sure that his apprentices were schooled in sound doctrine. The knowledge of the true is an insurance policy against the false. Part of the function of apostolic ministry is maintaining the purity of doctrine in the church and keeping the church and believers from being blown about by every wind of doctrine (see Ephesians 4:14).

Third, Paul focused on ministry philosophy (see Philippians 2:18-24). Paul was not just interested in his apprentices ministering what he ministered (content), he wanted them to minister in the same way that he ministered (spirit). Paul's ministry philosophy was based on a servant-leadership style that he wanted to duplicate in his followers.

Fourth, Paul focused on godly traditions (see 2 Thessalonians 3:6-7). Every family has certain traditions that make it unique. Paul understood that there were two kinds of traditions: bad traditions that hinder us from fulfilling the Word of God (see Mark 7:13), and good traditions or ways of doing things that help or assist us in fulfilling God's will. Paul wanted to pass these on to his sons in the faith and through them to subsequent generations.

Fifth, Paul focused on lifestyle (see 2 Thessalonians 3:7-9). Paul focused on character development, becoming faithful, living life as a God-pleaser, and being willing to defer his personal rights for the sake of the Gospel. Paul wanted these marks to be on his spiritual offspring. He wanted his offspring to share his value system and be made after his image.

4. *PROVIDING TRAINING EXPERIENCES.* As Jesus was preparing his followers to get along without Him, He provided them with training experiences. He gave them opportunities to function while He was present so that they would have confidence to function in His absence.

He sent the Twelve out two-by-two to test their wings (see Luke 9:1-2). At times, He let them experience failure (see Matthew 17:14-21). All of these experiences, both the positive ones and the negative ones became the lesson material of the day.

After each experience, Jesus used the experience as a means of instruction in what to do or in what not to do (see Luke 9:10). These real life experiences opened the hearts of the emerging apostles and gave them a readiness to learn.

By teaching in Bible school over twenty-five years, I have found that the students who come right out of high school are not necessarily the ones who are the most ready to learn. The ones who really get the most out of school are the ones who have had some experience and perhaps even failed. They usually have a greater appreciation for the teaching that they are getting because they understand how it relates to real life.

The mentor must work to find appropriate ministry opportunities that will help to develop the gifts and calling of God in his apprentice. Using Jesus' tests of faithfulness as a model, he should begin with smaller tasks to test the servant spirit. As they are faithful, more significant things can be assigned.

Apprentices may be given special projects that directly relate to their leadership call. A reporting back and a critical analysis of the experience should follow all projects or assignments. In this way, the mentor can assist the apprentice in extracting the most from each learning activity.

5. *ACCOUNTABILITY.* If true mentoring is to take place, no area of life can be off limits to the process. The mentor/apprentice relationship is one of accountability. This means that issues of character development, prayer life, family life, financial life, and other personal Christian disciplines must come under submission to God's Word.

    This means at times there must be a place for asking hard questions on a regular basis, coupled with a commitment to openness and honesty in the relationship. This is not for the purpose of prying or being nosy, but it is to assist the man or woman of God to reflect the message that they will bear.

6. *SHEPHERDING CARE.* Because of the history of the word "shepherding" in recent Christian experience, this word has become a synonym for "control." That is certainly not what Jesus meant when He said that He was a good shepherd. Many in the past have used the concept to get their disciples to serve them, when in Jesus' mind it was just the opposite.

To Jesus, being a shepherd meant that you were willing to lay your life down for the sheep (see John 10:11). This is how Jesus exercised His shepherding ministry and, evidently, we have been called to do the same (see 1 John 3:16).

Being a mentor must be seen as a selfless act on the part of the one doing the mentoring. It is much like raising children. I often tell people, "If you want to live a selfish life don't get married. Or if you are married, don't have children." Being committed to a spouse or bringing children into the world demands that we live for others—not for ourselves.

Ministries who want to live for themselves, live an uncomplicated existence, spend all they earn on their heart's desires, and live an isolated existence without much room for others will not succeed as mentors. To be a mentor, you must have a shepherd's heart that is willing to give your life for others.

Most of us would be willing to die for a stranger who was drowning by diving into the water to save them (especially if we did not have to think about it too long). That kind of heroism is usually more of a reflex action than a determined commitment. It is much more difficult to lay down your daily life (i.e. time, talent, and resources) for others.

Mentoring involves putting the life of others ahead of your own. It involves investing in a future from which you might not personally benefit. It involves making a place in your life for the annoying, the immature, and the just plain ornery.

7. *ENCOURAGEMENT AND EXHORTATION.* Every emerging ministry needs a mentor who will be open and honest. In addition, they need someone to believe in them.

Barnabas is such a good example of this. He was known for his spirit of encouragement. He was able to see things in people that no one else could see. He had eyes of faith for people and somehow was able to assist people in believing in themselves.

Mentoring has a lot to do with seeing the unseen and instilling a vision in the hearts of the apprentice. Yes, there should be an openness and honesty that deals realistically with real issues and real problems. But unless the mentor can inspire the apprentice to stretch toward the future, to the mark of the high calling in Christ, he will not be successful. In this sense, the mentor is like a good coach that is able to bring the best out of every player.

Not Many Fathers

It is not hard to see why Paul made the statement that you might have *"ten thousand instructors in Christ, yet you do not have many fathers"* (1 Corinthians 4:15). It is not easy to be a father. It is not easy to put your own agenda aside and live for others. It is not easy to put on the apron of humility, grab a towel, and wash the feet of the saints. But that is a big part of apostolic ministry.

Many people want the title of "father," but they do not all desire the function that goes with it. Having children is easy, being a real dad is something altogether different.

Apostolic ministry is all about fathering and serving. Jesus gave us a wonderful example of how to lay our lives down for others. Paul and Barnabas did the same thing as they gave themselves to the younger ministries they trained. Laying your life down requires a big commitment of time, talent and resources. I pray that many will be willing to pay the price for the sake of Christ and His kingdom and become fathering servants.

10

APOSTOLIC AUTHORITY

"Not that we have dominion over your faith, but are fellow workers for your joy; for by faith you stand."

(2 CORINTHIANS 1:24)

When we discuss the authority of an apostle, we soon discover a great divergence of viewpoints. Part of the reason for such divergence is due to what is said in Scripture itself. At one moment it appears that the ministry of the apostle is preeminent in relation to other ministries, and at the next moment it appears to be subservient to the other ministries.

This apparent contradiction makes this subject great fodder for animated debate. Depending on what position you would like to take on the issue of apostolic authority, you have some verses that seem to support your view. Unfortunately, most of those discussing the subject seem to take the view that the apostle is first on the list of ministries in the body of Christ.

Apostles First

Most people who see apostolic ministry on the top of a spiritual hierarchy use a few key verses. The principal one is found in 1 Corinthians 12:28-29. There Paul listed some of the ministries in the body of Christ and stated that *"God has appointed these in the church: first apostles, second prophets, third teachers, after that miracles, then gifts of healings, helps, administrations, varieties of tongues."*

Many have suggested that this is proof that apostles and prophets are over the churches and that they are, in a sense, superior in authority to the other body ministries. This is confirmed, they feel, by the listing of the five-fold ministries in Ephesians 4:11 where apostles and prophets are listed first.

Apostles Last

In contrast to this, Paul, at times, seems to give us quite a different look at the apostolic ministry. Instead of seeing apostles as first on a list of church functions, he seems to position apostles as last (see 1 Corinthians 4:9).

In fact, he says that as an apostle he is *"nothing"* (2 Corinthians 12:11), he is a *"servant"* (see 1 Corinthians 4:1), and he states that apostles in general have been made as *"the filth of the world, the offscouring of all things"* (1 Corinthians 4:13).

In this same context, apostles are viewed as condemned men, spectacles to the world, fools, weak, dishonored, thirsty, hungry, poorly clothed, beaten and homeless (see 1 Corinthians 4:9-13). Who would want to be one?

Which is It?

So which is it? Is an apostle the chief cook or the bottle washer? Is an apostle the head or the tail? Is an apostle the exalted father or the humble servant?

First of all, let me say that I do not believe there is a spiritual hierarchy in the body of Christ. I do not believe that one ministry is more important than another. I do not believe that one particular ministry rules or superintends over the other ministries.

When Paul was enumerating ministries in the body of Christ in 1 Corinthians 12, he was not making an exhaustive list to establish a pecking order in the body of Christ. The phrase *"first apostles"* cannot be seen as a list of priority or pre-eminence. (While the Greek word that is used in this passage at times means the first in priority, it does not always mean that and its specific use must be determined by the context and a comparison to other verses relating to the same theme.) The apostle does not sit on the top of the ministry totem pole. It is much simpler than that.

When Paul said, *"first apostles,"* he was merely numbering his list just like you or I would if we were going to name a few examples. (i.e. "When I go to the store I need to pick up first eggs, second milk, after that cereal, pasta, tomato sauce and lettuce.")

If this was meant to be an order of priority in the body of Christ, several ministries are notably absent from the list. Where do pastors fit in? Where do evangelists fit? Do they come after those with the gift of tongues? Or was this just meant to be a random list used for the purpose of example (see Luke 12:1; Romans 1:8; 1 Corinthians 11:18; James 3:17 where this same word is used)?

No Pecking Order

The truth of the matter is that there is no spiritual pecking order in the body of Christ. As far as God is concerned, every ministry in the body of Christ is equal in importance. Each ministry has equal value in the sight of the Lord, and no one ministry automatically submits to another ministry by virtue of what ministry they possess, no more than every woman must submit to every man by virtue of gender.

All ministries are to submit to the headship of Christ and to the authorities that God has placed in the local church. The authority in the local church is the eldership of the church (see Hebrews 13:17). There is no authority higher in the local church than the eldership of that church.

Paul's Attitude Toward Apostleship

This is confirmed by Paul's whole attitude toward apostleship. He did not see himself as a king or ruler over others. He makes this clear to the Corinthians when he indicates that he is not the lord over them or their faith, but he is a helper of their joy (see 2 Corinthians 1:24).

As a helper, he is there to serve. As a helper, he is one who is called along side of them to encourage and assist them in becoming all that they could become in God. As a helper, he existed for them, they did not exist for him.

As you study Paul's language in his Epistles, you cannot help but notice a significant contrast to some today who call themselves apostles.

Peter's Attitude Toward Apostleship

Peter seems to have had the same attitude to that of Paul. When he writes his letters, he comes to them as a fellow elder. He seems to deal severely with the notion that those in leadership are lords. He makes it clear that all leaders are servants who function not on the basis of what they can get, but on the basis of what they can give (see 1 Peter 5:1-5).

He is clear to put himself in this category when he opens his second epistle as *"a bondservant and apostle of Jesus Christ."* When he writes, he does not approach them with orders from the head. He reminds them of the things they have been taught (see 2 Peter 1:12; 3:1-2) and urges them to live a life worthy of their calling in God.

The Area of Rule

Does this mean that Peter and Paul did not exercise authority among the churches? Not at all! They had a great deal of authority and used it in a way that built up and edified the church.

The key to their authority was an understanding of their area of rule. Every ministry has an area of rule. As long as a ministry stays within that area of rule, they have great authority and freedom to function. As soon as they step outside of that area, or their God-ordained sphere, they cease to have authority.

The area of rule applies to two different issues. The first issue is that of calling. It is God who decides what ministry we will have. It is God who equips us with the gifts and graces necessary for function in the ministry to which He has called us. This is why Paul was so concerned that we evaluate our calling soberly and accurately (see Romans 12:3). When we are functioning within the parameters of God's calling, or our area of rule, we will find the grace, faith, and supernatural gifting that we need to minister. However, if we are trying to be something other than what God created us to be, we will not have the grace to succeed.

The second area of rule has to do with your specific responsibility within your prescribed area of ministry. You are a pastor, but to whom? You are an apostle, but to whom? Paul talked about this in 2 Corinthians 10:12-18. He talked about the sphere that was appointed to him by God. He reminds the Corinthian church that they were definitely a part of his sphere when he said, "I may not be an apostle to others, but I sure am a apostle to you" (see 1 Corinthians 9:2, my paraphrase).

The Sphere of Relationship

What made the Corinthian church part of Paul's sphere was his relationship to them. Paul had founded this church. The members of the leadership team of this church were his converts. He had laid his hands on them. He had been the one to disciple them and place them into their role of ministry. He was the spiritual father of this church and its leaders in the fullest sense of the word.

It was because of this relationship that Paul had authority. This was not a structural authority that belonged to him because his name was listed in the church by-laws as the apostle. It was a spiritual authority that was understood by virtue of Paul's past involvement and pastoral care in the church.

Paul understood the Corinthian church to be in his sphere of apostolic ministry. Just like the Galatian, Ephesian, Thessalonian, and Philippian churches were part of that same sphere. They were part of his rule because he had fathered these churches.

Paul understood that even though he was an apostle to these churches, it did not automatically make him an apostle to other churches. Why? Because his relationship to these other churches was different. An apostle to one is not an apostle to all. A ministry may be truly apostolic in nature, but everyone does not need to recognize that fact for the apostolic ministry to function in their God-ordained area of rule.

It is just like fatherhood. A father is always a father, but he is not a father to everyone who is a son. He is a father to his own sons and his own daughters. Just because I am a father, it does not give me authority in my neighbor's house with my neighbor's children. I cannot say to my neighbor's children, "I am a father, therefore, you must obey me." That would be ridiculous! All children are not subject to every father no more than all churches or leaders are to be subject to everyone who calls themselves an apostle.

There is no authority without relationship. Paul had a special relationship with the churches that he established. He had a personal relationship with the leadership team of these churches and he knew many of the members intimately. In his greetings he often expressed deep love for those to whom he is writing.

This love that Paul had for his audience is the reason Paul can speak like he does. Notice his heart of love as he addresses the churches:

> *"For out of much affliction and anguish of heart I wrote to you, with many tears, not that you should be grieved, but that you might know the love which I have so abundantly for you."* (2 CORINTHIANS 2:4)

> *"I thank my God upon every remembrance of you...."* (PHILIPPIANS 1:3)

> *"...I have you in my heart...."* (PHILIPPIANS 1:7)

> *"For God is my witness, how greatly I long for you all with the affection of Jesus Christ."* (PHILIPPIANS 1:8)

> *"Therefore, my beloved and longed-for brethren, my joy and crown...."* (PHILIPPIANS 4:1)

> *"So, affectionately longing for you, we were well pleased to impart to you not only the Gospel of God, but also our own lives, because you had become dear to us."* (1 THESSALONIANS 2:8)

Paul had this special love for all of the churches that he established. He continually refers to the people in these churches as *"beloved"* (2 Thessalonians 2:13) and *"brethren"* (Philippians 3:1). He refers to the leadership of the churches as his sons in the Gospel (2 Timothy 1:2) and true companions (see Philippians 4:3).

Paul's Ministry to his Churches

For this reason, Paul ministered differently when he was in a situation that involved his area of rule than when he was not. When Paul wrote to the churches that he personally established, the content of his letter was completely different from when he wrote to churches that he did not father.

When he wrote to the Corinthian church, for instance, he came across fairly strong. He pleaded with them (see 1 Corinthians 1:10), rebuked them for their carnality (see 3:1-4), warned them (see 4:18ff.), told them what to do (see 5:3-5), and even threatened them (see 4:21). He reminded them that he planted this church (see 3:6) and they were his work in the Lord (see 9:1).

In addition, he was quite personal in his admonitions to specific people in the congregation. In the church at Philippi, evidently some of his appointed leaders were not getting along so well. Paul exhorted them to, "get their act together" (see Philippians 4:2, my paraphrase).

These were not strangers to Paul. These were his spiritual kids, he had given birth to them (see 1 Corinthians 4:15) and he was not afraid to be bold in his instruction. They were part of his area of rule and, just as with a natural father, God would hold him accountable for how he handled his own offspring. For this reason, while Paul mentions his apostleship in most of his letters, he defends it only in the churches that he founded.

It should be noted here that while Paul was strong with these churches at times, he always respected the authority of the leadership of these churches. Paul fully intended that his letters be read to the entire congregation (see 1 Thessalonians 5:27), but he sent his letters to the senior pastors of the congregations (see Philippians 4:3). Those senior pastors had total control over whether anyone in the congregation would ever see Paul's letter. He followed the pattern of Jesus, who wrote letters to the seven churches of Asia in the Book of Revelation. Jesus sent those messages to the *angelos* of the churches (see Revelation 2:1,8,12,18; 3:1,7,14).

In addition, Paul clearly saw his authority emanating from the Word of God. When he was standing on solid biblical ground, he was not afraid to be very direct and forceful in his instruction. However, when Paul had no clear Scripture behind him, he was careful to let them know that this was his opinion and that he was giving advice and suggested guidelines rather than commandments (see 1 Corinthians 7; 2 Corinthians 8:10).

Paul's Ministry to Other Churches

Paul's ministry to churches that he did not establish was quite different. The book of Romans is a good example here (and the book of Hebrews, if you believe that Paul was the author). In writing to the Romans, Paul introduced himself as a *"bondservant of Jesus Christ"* (Romans 1:1).

In this book, Paul gave no rebukes or personal admonitions. He greeted the people that he knew and introduced them to others, but the whole tenor of the book is different. Paul instead focused on theology and spoke to them in general terms.

Paul understood that as he wrote to the believers at the church in Rome, he was in a different sphere. He was not in his specific area of rule. The level of his authority changed and he did not take liberties with another man's flock. In fact, he functioned more as a teacher than an apostle.

The book of Colossians is also written to a church that Paul did not found. This book is more direct than the book of

Romans and Paul deals with some specific issues in this church. Is there a contradiction here? The answer is, "No there is not."

While Paul did not found the Colossian church, he was writing the letter at the encouragement of the person who had—a man by the name of Epaphras (see Colossians 1:7). Paul had never actually been to the Colossian church in person (see 2:1). But while he was under house arrest in Rome, evidently Epaphras came to Paul with some concerns about the church.

Epaphras appreciated Paul's knowledge of the Word and his ability to communicate through letters. He had tried to adjust the church without much success and he was calling upon Paul to help him out. Paul obliged him and wrote to the Colossian church at the request and with full approval of the man who was the spiritual father of the church (see Colossians 4:12-13).

Paul's Respect for Lines of Authority

When Paul worked with others, he always did so with authority in mind. He understood that he had spiritual authority, but he did not want to abuse that authority (see 1 Corinthians 9:18). He was always careful to acknowledge and work through other God-ordained authority. It did not matter whether Paul was dealing with a church or an individual, Paul was very careful not to step out of his area of rule. He was very careful to honor proper authority. He refused to usurp authority or step into another person's sphere (see 2 Corinthians 10:12-18).

This was not only demonstrated in his relationship with the Colossian church, but it was also demonstrated in his treatment of Onesimus. Onesimus was a slave who had run away from his master Philemon. Somehow he had ended up in Rome and had a divine encounter with Paul in Rome. However it happened, Paul had the opportunity to lead this runaway slave to Christ (see Philemon 10). Paul had evidently grown quite fond of Onesimus, but he knew that if Onesimus' repentance was going to be complete, he would have to return to his master.

This was difficult for Paul, but he only had to read some of his own letters to know what had to be done (see Ephesians 6:5-8). Paul respected Philemon's authority over his own slave and sent Onesimus back to him with a personal letter in his hand that asked Philemon to show mercy on this slave who was now a brother in Christ.

The Apostle and the Elders

Both Peter and Paul serve as good examples of apostles who had great respect for the leadership of the local church. Neither of them felt that they were above the leaders of the church. Both of them confirmed the authority of the local leaders and sought to encourage others to also respond properly to authority.

The writer to the Hebrews indicated how important it is for every believer to have proper respect and relationship to elders. The writer indicated that believers should walk in a submitted relationship to the authorities that have been placed in their lives (see Hebrews 13:17).

In Paul's early years, he ministered at the Antioch church with Barnabas. He did not go out in his apostolic function until the local church leaders had confirmed his call and were willing to lay their hands on him and send him out.

Paul went with a sense of commissioning from both the Lord and his home church. After each missionary journey, he returned home and gave an account of his trip, which I am sure was a great encouragement to the home church. Between missionary journeys, it appears that he rolled up his sleeves and became a functioning part of the local church. Some expositors feel that there could have been as much as a three to five year furlough between one of his trips.

Peter functioned the same way. In his day-to-day function, he appeared to have viewed himself as one of the elders (see 1 Peter 5:1). He functioned in the Jerusalem church, with many of the other apostles, right next to the elders. In fact, it appears that the twelve apostles were a functioning part of the Jerusalem eldership.

Apostles are not leaders without authority in their lives. They must be in right relationship to a local church eldership just like every other ministry in the body of Christ. They must give an account for their actions just like every other ministry in the body of Christ. They must follow the same guidelines that they give to others.

Some ministries today function with no local church covering. They give lip service to the concept of being under authority by gathering a group of handpicked, unrelated ministries to form a phantom board that seldom meets. When they are asked, they say that they are accountable to this board they have put together. But in reality, they are an authority to themselves.

The checks and balances for all ministries are found in the local church. No ministry is exempt from their need to be accountable. It does not matter if God has called you to be an apostle, a prophet, or an evangelist, He wants you to be under the authority of a local church eldership.

Authority for Edification

Paul understood that he had been given authority by God to function in his area of rule. This authority was a tool for him to use to build the church (see 2 Corinthians 13:10). He used it to build the church, not to promote himself or build up his ministry.

In fact, when it came to his rights as an apostle, he usually deferred them for the sake of the Gospel. He had the true heart of a father. A father seeks to bless rather than how he might be blessed.

He had every right to receive financial support from the churches he had planted, but more often than not he deferred that right so that his intentions would not be misread (see 1 Corinthians 9:12,15,18; 2 Corinthians 12:14-15).

Paul truly functioned with the heart of a father. His authority was not something that he used for himself, it was something that made it possible for him to raise up spiritual offspring and bring them into a place of independence and fruitfulness.

There is no hierarchy of ministries in the body of Christ. Every ministry, regardless of title, is important to the success of the whole. If the body of Christ is to fulfill its destiny all ministries must flow together, be under proper authority, experience a call from God, and function in their God-ordained area of rule. When they do this, they will experience the impartation of faith, grace, and divine gifting that is necessary to fulfill their destiny.

11

AN
APOSTOLIC
CHURCH

"And you became followers of us and of the Lord, having received the word in much affliction, with joy of the Holy Spirit, so that you became examples to all in Macedonia and Achaia, who believe. For from you the word sounded forth, not only in Macedonia and Achaia, but also in every place."

(1 THESSALONIANS 1:6-8A)

In one sense, we could say that the church in Antioch was the first church Paul started. Even though the church actually began prior to Paul's coming to assist Barnabas, it was Paul's persecution of the church that caused the scattering of believers from Jerusalem to other cities like Antioch (see Acts 8:1).

As these believers were scattered, they went everywhere preaching the Word and sharing their faith (see Acts 8:4). They primarily reached out to other Jews (see Acts 11:19). Some of these believers whose original roots were in Cyprus and Cyrene, however, journeyed to Antioch and were more open to preaching the Gospel to a more diverse crowd (see Acts 11:20). As they preached, many people turned to the Lord (see Acts 11:21).

Soon the news of this revival reached the church at Jerusalem and the leaders of the Jerusalem church decided to send leadership to Antioch to formulate this loose-knit group of converts into a local church (see Acts 11:22).

But whom should they send? Who would be a likely candidate to bring order and structure to this move of the Spirit that was taking place among the Hellenists in Antioch? The Jerusalem leaders selected Barnabas, a good man who was full of the Holy Spirit and faith, and who had been a faithful man in the local church for many years (see Acts 11:24 with Acts 4:36-37). Not only was Barnabas a good choice because of his faithfulness and character, he was a good choice because of his natural connection and familiarity with the culture of those in that region (see Acts 11:20 with Acts 4:36).

When Barnabas arrived, he quickly realized he had his work cut out for him. He experienced a great wave of evangelism as he preached the Word. He realized that he was going to need some help rooting and grounding these converts in the faith and shaping them into a pattern church (see Acts 11:24-25).

Where would he go to find such help? As he prayed about it, he remembered a man that he had befriended a long time ago by the name of Saul (see Acts 9:27). He was a man who was thoroughly schooled in the Scripture and would be able to teach the Word of God to these converts. Barnabas went looking for this man, Saul.

Barnabas and Saul became a team, and for the next few years they intensely taught the people. Not only would they work as a team in the new church, they would become the first missionaries to be sent out from this church in order to fulfill their apostolic call (see Acts 13:1-3).

History and Background of the Antioch Church

This is how the church at Antioch was started. This church was destined to become a very influential church for well over 500 years. Some of the giants among the early church fathers pastored this great church, including Ignatius of Antioch who was most likely the third senior pastor of this church.

This church began like all churches. It started out as a small church with little or no influence in its city. However, because the foundation of this church was strong and the nature of the lifestyle of the people that made up this church was truly Christian, the church grew strong and became quite influential. In fact, this church at its height grew to a congregation of over 100,000 in membership with over 3,000 people on paid staff. [5]

Because of the Jewish nature of the Jerusalem church, and because of the destruction of Jerusalem in A.D. 70, it is fair to say that the church at Antioch became the first church to really model true New Testament Christianity. In doing so, it became the pattern church for the world. It still serves us today as a pattern for an apostolic church.

The church of Antioch had been birthed out of an apostolic ministry and it went on to fulfill an apostolic call as a congregation. The key elements in the foundation of this church, as it is described in the book of Acts, serve as a model for apostolic churches in the world today. What were these key elements that established the Antioch church as an apostolic church? What are the characteristics of a modern-day Antioch church?

Twelve Characteristics of an Antioch Church

The Antioch church was:

1. *AN EVANGELISTIC CHURCH (SEE ACTS 11:19-20).* The Antioch church was started by believers who were fleeing for their lives, but could not cease to share the Good News wherever they went. These were people who had been delivered from the kingdom of darkness and were ready to risk their lives to bring others into that same experience of freedom. The Antioch church was birthed in a spirit of evangelism.

   This spirit of evangelism continued under the ministry of Barnabas and Saul. So often churches that begin evangelistic lose the evangelistic edge as they get to a certain size. Much of the church growth in North America today simply consists of believers moving from one church to another.

   Fortunately, there were no other churches in Antioch when Barnabas came to that city. If the church was to grow, it had to grow through evangelism. An apostolic church is a church that is able to keep the fires of evangelism alive, even though the church may be many years old. Reaching our own Jerusalem is still the first commission to the church (see Acts 1:8).

2. *A TEACHING CHURCH (SEE ACTS 11:26; 13:1).* The Antioch church was a church committed to the intense training and discipleship of its membership. Paul and Barnabas taught intensely. They believed and practiced the commission that Jesus had given in Matthew's account (see Matthew 28:18-20). When new converts came into the church there was a discipleship track for them to run on.

If a congregation of people is ever going to get to the place where they are touching the world, they are going to have to be composed of disciplined believers.

Disciplined believers have done more than pray a simple prayer at their conversion. Disciplined believers have sold out to the lordship of Jesus Christ and made a radical change in how they live. Disciplined believers have put the purposes of God ahead of their own purposes, and have left houses and lands for the sake of the Gospel.

Members of an Antioch church must be true disciples who have come to the cross, repented of their sins, accepted the life of faith, been baptized in water and the Holy Spirit, and have distinguished themselves from the sinful generation in which they live (see Acts 2:38-40). The members of an Antioch church will be expected to make personal sacrifices to see the harvest become a reality.

In order to produce these types of disciples, the Antioch church must be a place of systematic teaching from the Word of God. Church leaders and members must place a high priority on being taught and equipped. This means teaching must be woven into the fabric of church life.

Paul and Barnabas focused on teaching as they laid the foundation of this great church. They taught for change and witnessed a change in the lives of the people. The character of Jesus was produced in them to the point that they were called Christians because their life reflected the character and nature of Christ, not because they merely attended church services on Sunday (see Acts 11:26).

As Barnabas and Paul were faithful to teach, other teachers were raised up. In fact, by the time Barnabas and Paul were ready to be sent out as the first missionaries of this church, they had replaced themselves. Acts 13:1 tells us that there were certain *"prophets and teachers"* in Antioch. Where did these leaders come from? They came out of the teaching ministry of Paul and the prophetic ministry of Barnabas.

History records that leaders from the Antioch church were used to help maintain doctrinal purity in the emerging church and that it established a theological seminary to train church leaders for many years to come.[6]

3. *A MULTI-RACIAL CHURCH (SEE ACTS 11:20; 13:1).* As you look at the complexion of the leadership team at the Antioch church it is immediately apparent that this church was a blending of races and cultures—much more than Jerusalem could ever have been. Those who founded this church had a very inclusive vision and extended the Gospel beyond the Jewish community—including men of Cyprus and Cyrene (Northern Africa). Their leadership included Lucius of Cyrene.

This kind of diversity does not usually happenstance in church planting. Too many church planters and church builders limit the scope of their vision. Actually, the more diverse the church is, the more powerful and influential it will become. We want the church to be just as diverse as the throngs gathered before the throne of God in the book of Revelation.

The various races and ethnic backgrounds represent our Samaria and needs to be a focal point of ministry and outreach. God loves all people of all nations and He does not want our heart to be any smaller (see Deuteronomy 10:17-19).

An Antioch church begins by reaching out to the nations in its own backyard. Today, many communities have large ethnic populations. Many of these people are immigrants to this country and are strangers and foreigners in our midst. God is clear in His admonitions that we are not to forget the stranger or the foreigners among us, but we are to open our hearts to them.

Building a church with wide ethnic diversity actually paves the way for touching the nations of the world. How can we expect to love the people of the world that we have not seen when we find it so difficult to love those same people that we see every day in our own communities?

4. *A TEAM MINISTRY CHURCH (SEE ACTS 13:1)*. The Antioch church believed in the five-fold ministry and practiced team ministry. The leadership of the church was a broad-based leadership team where all of the leadership gifts were present. The evangelistic gift, the prophetic gift, the teaching gift, the pastoral gift, and the apostolic gift were all in evidence and operation.

As a result, all of the ministries of the body of Christ could be identified and the various gifts among them could then be adequately equipped and released. Team ministry makes it possible for the leadership to reproduce after its own kind. Churches that do not have a healthy pipeline of up-and-coming ministries will have a difficult time sending ministries forth. It was because Paul and Barnabas replaced themselves that they could be sent out by the Antioch church without fear that the mother church would be in peril.

If team ministry is a concept that is new to you, I recommend that you read *Team Ministry* by Dick Iverson. In that book, he shares his personal journey in team ministry and includes guidelines for developing and releasing a team.

5. *A SPIRIT-ANOINTED CHURCH (SEE ACTS 13:2).* The Antioch church believed and practiced the gifts of the Spirit. The gifts of the Spirit enumerated in 1 Corinthians 12 are definite supernatural gifts given by the Holy Spirit to assist the church in accomplishing its mission. They flow along with the power promised through the baptism of the Holy Spirit (see Acts 1:8).

It is a terrible thing to have the character of Jesus without His power. Both are needed. If we have the power of God without the character of Christ we will be dangerous. But if we have the character of Christ without His supernatural power, we will be powerless to fulfill the ministry that our heart of compassion demands.

The Antioch church had a perfect balance of the fruit of the Spirit and the gifts of the Spirit, and had a special touch of the grace of God on all that they did. There was healing, deliverance, and prophetic gifts in operation.

If Jesus is truly going to be the head of the church, there must be a way for Him to communicate to His people. One of the ways that the Spirit speaks in the church is through the prophetic word. The prophetic word came to the church at Antioch, *"Now separate to*

Me Barnabas and Saul for the work to which I have called them" (Acts 13:2).

This was not just a word for Barnabas and Saul; it was a word for the church as well. The church was required pay the ultimate price as an apostolic church—they had to be willing to send out apostolic ministries to function in their call.

6. *A PROPHETIC CHURCH (SEE ACTS 11:27-30; 13:2).* The Antioch church made a strong place for prophecy in the church. Jesus was the head of this church and His voice, as heard through prophecy, was important in guiding and directing the mission of the church. As a result, it became a place where prophets were raised up and their ministry was respected.

When Agabus visited this people, he had liberty to share his prophetic gift. As he shared a prediction about a famine that was to come some years later, there was an immediate response to the word. The church sent relief to Jerusalem for a famine that would not actually happen for five to seven years.

The members of the Antioch church had what is sometimes referred to as 20/20 prophetic vision based on 2 Chronicles 20:20.

"Believe in the Lord your God, and you shall be established; believe His prophets, and you will prosper."
(2 CHRONICLES 20:20B)

Paul and Barnabas deserve credit for discipling this group of believers. They respected the word of the Lord and were willing to do whatever the Lord asked of them, no matter how costly it may have been. That is the spirit of an Antioch church—instant obedience.

7. *A GENEROUS CHURCH (SEE ACTS 11:30 13:3)*. The Antioch church was a giving church. They had truly experienced the Scripture, *"It is more blessed to give than to receive"* (Acts 20:35). An apostolic church must have a generous spirit. Missionary work, planting churches, reaching out in evangelism, and providing training programs for future leaders all cost money.

It is so much easier to just sit, relax, and be a nice little community church that hangs on until Jesus comes. But if a church is going to be a city, nation, and world-influencing church, it needs to be a church filled with people who love the people of the world more than they do their own money, comfort, or pleasure.

An Antioch church is a church with a high level of commitment among its membership. It is a church where people are willing to expend their time, talent, and resources. It is a place where they are willing to give their best away.

I remember talking to one pastor who had just sent out one of his elders to plant a church in a nearby community. This church plant had been scheduled for some time and several of the families of the church were planning on being a part of it.

Everything was fine until after the new church had been planted. Suddenly, the mother church realized a new lack. They missed the elder who had gone and the families who had gone with him. The church plant was a success, but there was a hole in their heart.

The mother church went through a grieving process as if they had actually lost a loved one. The pastor asked me to come and share with the congregation on the cost of church planting. Church planting sometimes takes your very best.

In my own experience over the years, I have been part of a leadership team that believed and practiced church planting. During this process, I have lost many of my very closest friends to the field as they followed the call of God on their lives. It was a painful, yet glorious experience. At least now I can go almost anywhere in the world and get free lodging.

There is a cost to being an apostolic church. The cost includes the sacrifice of time, talent, and finances. It includes saying goodbye to friends and family who join with others in team outreaches. It includes being willing to let go of pastors and church leaders that we have grown to love and appreciate. It even means seeing your senior pastor move out of his or her position and become more apostolic in nature. It means being willing to share your leadership with the world.

I have been a part of an apostolic church since 1972. I came to Bible Temple (now City Bible Church) in Portland, Oregon to go to Portland Bible College and have been there ever since. I have served under the pastoral and apostolic leadership of Dick Iverson and later Frank Damazio.

I have to say that many times I thought it would be nice to be in church that was more laid back. But now, as I see the fruit of this church all over the world, I realize that whatever the cost has been, it has been well worth it.

8. *A WORSHIPPING CHURCH (SEE ACTS 13:2)*. The Antioch church was a church that understood their function as priests unto God. They knew how to minister unto the Lord. The ministry unto the Lord in this passage undoubtedly refers to an atmosphere of worship. As priests unto God, one of our primary functions is minis-

tering to the Lord. We minister to the Lord through our sacrifices of praise and worship.

New Testament priests who understand their God-ordained function to position themselves in worship are also the kind of people who can be led and directed by the Holy Spirit. Our posture of worship places us in a position to hear the voice of the Lord more clearly.

If Jesus is going to be the builder of the church, the people of the church must be in a place of humility before the Lord that allows them to receive His instruction. Our posture of worship is a continual reminder that Jesus is the Lord of the church.

9. A PRAYING CHURCH (SEE ACTS 13:3). The Antioch church made it a priority to set aside seasons of prayer and fasting. Prayer is the pipeline of the Spirit and was a major key to the success of the church in the book of Acts. A praying church is a powerful church.

An apostolic church must be composed of people who know how to touch God in their personal life, who know how to get the mind of the Spirit in seasons of prayer, and who are seasoned enough to know what comes from God and what does not.

An apostolic church also fosters a corporate prayer life among its members. This would include regular prayer among the elders and leaders of the church, corporate prayer times in the regular life and activity of the church, and special seasons of prayer, fasting, and waiting on God.

It is in these seasons of prayer and fasting that God often speaks to the church as a whole and gives the church His agenda. I know each year we try to begin the year with a Solemn Assembly to posture ourselves to receive God's agenda for the coming year.

10. *AN EQUIPPING CHURCH.* The Antioch church believed that the primary function of leaders was to raise up, equip, and release the body of Christ for ministry (see Ephesians 4:11-12). They believed that every member had a function in the church and were committed to seeing every believer reach their destiny.

   Leaders of apostolic churches cannot be jealous leaders who suppress other would-be leaders in the church. They need to have confidence in their own calling in God and be willing to acknowledge the gifts and ministries in others. They will find joy in seeing others reach ministry goals and destiny.

   The Antioch church believed in the laying on of hands for commissioning. They also believed in prophetic gatherings for the confirmation of calling.

11. *A WORLD CHURCH.* I am sure that the Antioch church had a vision for their city, but they also had a vision for the world. Antioch became the center for world missions and church planting teams. The book of Acts only gives us the record of one of these teams, but we know that there were other teams doing the same thing. Paul and Barnabas began as the first team. Later they split up and there were two teams, Paul and Silas, and Barnabas and John Mark (see Acts 15:39-40).

   Apostolic churches use Acts 1:8 as their pilot verse. They have a vision for Jerusalem, or their city. They have a vision for Judea, or their region. They have a vision for Samaria, which includes other ethnic groups within their sphere of influence. But they also have a vision for the world. They believe in world missionary activity that takes the Gospel to the uttermost parts of the earth.

12. *A RESPECTED CHURCH.* The Antioch church became respected as a model for New Testament Christianity. It became a pattern for other churches to follow. It became a place where church disputes were settled. Several church councils were held in Antioch and it was considered one of the top five churches in the world for many centuries to follow.

What a tremendous church! How does a church get to this place of prominence and influence? How does a church become an apostolic church?

The Foundation of the Antioch Church

A tremendous church must be built on a good foundation. The foundation of the Antioch church must be in place if any church is going to pattern themselves after this early church.

The foundation of the Antioch church involved five things to which I have already alluded. All five of these deal with the quality of Christianity that was experienced by the membership of this great church. The greatness of a church is not measured by the quality of its leaders, but by the quality of the average member who belongs to the church. Here are the five components of an Antioch church foundation:

1. *A TURNING TO THE LORD (SEE ACTS 11:20-21).* When converts were added to the Lord in the Antioch church, there was a true turning. There was a turning away from sin and a turning unto the Lord. The Bible refers to this process as repentance. Repentance involves a 180-degree turn. You cannot turn to the Lord unless you turn from something else. New Testament Christianity involves a turning from darkness to light; a turning from serving self to serving the living God.

Turning to the Lord also involves coming into right relationship with Jesus Christ as the Lord of our lives. The believers at Antioch turned to the Lord. When we accept His lordship, we acknowledge that He is the Lord of the universe and over all. People loved the blessings and miracles of Jesus, but when it came to the matter of Lordship, they cried, *"We will not have this man reign to over us"* (Luke 19:14).

2. *A CLEAVING WITH PURPOSE OF HEART TO THE LORD (SEE ACTS 11:23).* The type of believers that formed the foundation of the Antioch church did not have a shallow commitment to the work of the local church. I do not want to speak ill of the seeker sensitive approach to Christianity because I think we need to remove any obstacles that may hinder people coming to Christ. However, people still must squarely face the obstacle of the cross and come to a complete surrender to Christ if they are going to be productive Christians.

Other translations of Barnabas' admonition to these believers include:

"To make up their minds to be faithful to the Master." – T C N T

"To be resolute and steadfast in their devotion to the Lord." – G D S P D

Barnabas was asking for a determination based on vision. Their faith was not just another thing that they were involved with, it was the center of their life. The word "cleave" means "to glue to; to attach oneself closely to." In Greek, it is descriptive of the relationship between husband and wife. God is looking for a covenant relationship among His people.

3. *A WILLINGNESS TO BE TAUGHT (SEE ACTS 11:26)*. The believers at Antioch had a hunger for the Word. Satisfying this hunger meant going to meetings—gathering themselves together. They were training together and searching the Scriptures daily. Christ and the church were their whole life.

I fully understand the concept of balance, but we may be so balanced that we will never move. In today's context, the question becomes, is the church imposing itself to expect more than one gathering a week? The people in the Antioch church viewed themselves as disciples—or pupils and learners. This implies humility on their part and a recognition that they needed what the Word of God provided.

Sometimes I do not think people are to blame for their own lack of appetite for the Word. If the people are not given opportunities to give out, and are not challenged to give of what they have, they will be too full and refuse to eat. But if the church is mobilized and released to function regularly, they will be eager for more.

4. *A RESPONSIVENESS TO THE LORD (SEE ACTS 11:27-29)*. It is beautiful the way these Christians at Antioch responded to the word of the Lord. The prophet prophesied a famine that was several years off and they determined to immediately send relief. They did not even wait for the famine to come. I am sure the people of Jerusalem were amazed to get an offering for a famine that they had not as yet experienced. We likely would have at least waited until the famine came and gathered interest on our money in the meantime.

But this was the heart of the Antioch church. They had a simple obedience to the voice of the Lord. There is no question that God would be able to lead them into many exploits. Too many of us resist the will of God and find it hard to respond to His leading. A church is no stronger than the people who make it up. Are we responsive and obedient? Can the Lord easily lead us?

5. *A GENUINE CHRISTIANITY (SEE ACTS 11:26).* It is important to note that the believers in Antioch were called Christians. They did not call themselves Christians. No buttons, badges, or bumper stickers gave signal to their faith. They were called Christians because the life they lived reminded observers of a person about whom they had some knowledge. These believers reminded people of Christ.

   A Christian is a follower of Christ. God is looking for people of faith who are willing to walk where Jesus walked in every aspect of life. The members of the Antioch church were good Christians first and part of an apostolic church second.

The Need Today

Every community has the need for an Antioch church. God wants many churches to accept the call and unique challenge to be an Antioch church for their region. God wants us all to lift our vision higher and see the world the way He does. He wants us to renew our passion for the commission.

QUESTIONS AND ANSWERS

In recent years I have traveled a lot throughout the world ministering primarily to pastors and other church leaders. As I go from place to place and country to country, I hear a lot of questions being posed about apostolic ministry and some of the practices that are being witnessed in the world today. I would like to use this chapter to answer some of the most commonly asked questions on apostolic ministry that I have encountered.

Sixteen Common Questions Concerning Apostolic Ministry:

1. *I HAVE HEARD APOSTOLIC MINISTRY TAUGHT IN AN ENTIRELY DIFFERENT WAY TO SUPPORT AN ENTIRELY DIFFERENT STYLE OF MINISTRY. HOW DO WE KNOW WHAT THE RIGHT TEACHING IS IN THIS AREA?*

This is a good question and the answer to this question and other questions like it is linked to your understanding of the Bible and its place in determining the doctrine and practice of the church. Is the Bible the final authority in all matters of doctrine? Does the Bible give us the pattern for this and other ministries? How much liberty can we take with the Bible?

I am fully aware that there is room for legitimate difference of interpretation of the Scripture. I am more concerned when there really is no attempt made to discover the biblical meaning through honest research.

There are some who seem to want to construct their own definitions to this ministry. They often use experience to confirm their view. Many times, these individuals who are trying to bolster their view will indicate that God has shown them certain things by anointing or revelation. The anointing does not free us to improvise or stretch ourselves beyond the Scripture. All revelation must be tested by the revelation found in the Word of God, the Bible.

I am not saying that apostolic ministry will not take on a variety of expressions. It will. There was great variety among the apostolic ministries named in the New Testament. The area where there seems to be the most abuse is in the area of apostolic authority. Apostolic ministries that are not rightly related to true biblical authority are dangerous.

2. *IS EVERY APOSTLE A CHURCH-PLANTING APOSTLE OR ARE THERE OTHER KINDS?*

As I just stated, apostolic ministry will have many faces. Certainly, one of the most common forms of apostolic ministry is that of church planting. Paul referred to himself as a *"master builder"* (1 Corinthians 3:10). The Greek word there is *arkitekton*. It is the word from which we get the word "architect." It refers to someone who oversees the erection of a building.

While not every apostle will be a church-planting apostle in the sense that they go from place to place starting churches as Paul did, the ultimate fruit of every apostolic ministry should be the existence of strong, reproducing local churches.

Whether this means that the apostle physically started each church is not the issue. The apostle may have mentored and sent out the ministries who physically started the churches. The apostle may have effectively equipped others to build a house according to God's pattern. In any case, the existence of these churches is a proof of apostleship.

3. *THE BIBLE OFTEN SPEAKS OF APOSTLES AND PROPHETS TOGETHER,*
DO THESE MINISTRIES HAVE A SPECIAL RELATIONSHIP TO EACH
OTHER?

It does appear from the Scripture that apostles and prophets have a special relationship in laying the foundation of the church and of local churches.

First of all, we see the Old Testament prophets and the twelve apostles of the Lamb involved in establishing the foundation of the eternal or universal church. Paul referred to this in Ephesians 2:19-22. He talked about the new house that God is building out of both Jews and Gentiles. This house, or holy temple, is the church.

He indicated that this building is built on the foundation of the apostles and prophets. These ministries laid that foundation through their preparation for the coming church Age. The twelve apostles laid the foundation of doctrine in the church (see Acts 2:42). In addition, they continually used the prophets of the Old Testament to confirm and affirm what God was doing in and among them (see Acts 2:17-21, 25-28). Jesus Himself used the prophets to verify His story (see Luke 24:27).

Beyond this, however, the new order of apostles and prophets established after Christ's ascension and exaltation seems to be linked by their work together in local churches. Ephesians 3:5 seems to be speaking of this new order of apostles and prophets.

It is interesting that Paul the apostle always felt more comfortable in ministry when a prophetic ministry accompanied him. On his first missionary journey, he was teamed up with Barnabas. Even though we have discussed Barnabas as an apostle as well, he seems to have many of the characteristics you would find in a prophetic ministry. The ministry of a prophet may have been his primary gift before moving into apostolic function.

This may be why Barnabas sought Saul from Tarsus to help teach and ground the new converts at Antioch as they shaped them into a solid apostolic church. Evidently, Barnabas was more prophetic in nature. This is evidenced by his strong gift of encouragement (see Acts 4:36) and exhortation (see Acts 11:23). The fruit that was produced under his ministry in the Antioch church further evidences it. We know that "like begets like." Paul, the teacher, and Barnabas, the prophet, produced prophets and teachers (see Acts 13:1).

Later on, when Paul embarked on his second missionary journey, he chose Silas to go with him. Silas was a prophet from the Jerusalem church that Paul had most likely met during the Jerusalem council (see Acts 15:22,32).

There is no question that Paul believed in team ministry when it came to carrying out his apostolic call. In fact, it appears that he was reluctant to minister with great freedom and boldness in the absence of other ministries (see Acts 18:4-5).

No one wants to stereotype ministries. But there is no question that God uses a variety of ministries to provide checks, balances, and security to each other. God has made us all different. By nature of their call, prophets must be very sensitive to the leading of the Holy Spirit. They are often dramatic in their revelations, and strong in exhortation and vision. This is very important in apostolic ministry and church planting.

Apostles, on the other hand, will tend to be more practical, more matter of fact, more cut and dried and strategic in how they approach things. Paul understood his own personal need for balance. He did not just gather around him those who were most like him. He realized that a suitable help to him would most likely be his opposite.

This is a lot like marriage. Although we want to be careful once again about stereotypes, women and men tend to be opposites in many areas. That is what makes them a good match. No one has all of the grace and ability needed to be all things to all men. Therefore, God gives us suitable help.

The prophet is a suitable help to the apostle. They complement each other and provide a church with a well-balanced ministry.

4. *PAUL TALKS ABOUT THE SIGNS OF AN APOSTLE. HE MENTIONS SIGNS AND WONDERS. DO ALL APOSTLES FUNCTION IN SIGNS AND WONDERS?*

Often, the verse in 2 Corinthians 12:12 is used as a text to suggest that apostles must move freely in signs and wonders. The suggestion is that if the person does not have a miracle ministry, perhaps he or she is not an apostle after all. They may have planted 100 churches, but if they do not perform signs and wonders, they must not be an apostle.

I certainly do not want to let any would-be apostle off from the desire or need to see signs and wonders displayed in their ministry. We know that signs and wonders should be the mark of the church of Jesus Christ. The presence of the supernatural is one of the things that should distinguish the church from other charitable and social organizations.

The fact is that all believers are to operate in signs and wonders (see Mark 16:17). Paul did function in signs, wonders, and mighty deeds (see Romans 15:18-20). Peter had signs and wonders follow him (see Acts 5:12-16). Philip, the evangelist, was used in signs and wonders in Samaria (see Acts 8:6). Stephen, one of the seven deacons, operated in signs and wonders as well (see Acts 6:8).

There is no question that God-anointed ministries should function in the power and authority of the Holy Spirit. All ministries should desire to be used of God to break spiritual bondage, set captives free, and bring healing, deliverance, and strength to those who sit in the chains of darkness.

The question is, does an apostle need to have signs and wonders as a key element of their ministry to be able to claim apostleship? Are signs and wonders the proof of his apostleship? I would have to say that it is impossible to tell with certainty from 2 Corinthians 12:12 alone.

There are two possible ways in which this verse can be translated. One way suggests that the signs and wonders were part of Paul's verification or proof of apostleship. This way is best exemplified in the *New International Version*, which says, *"The things that mark an apostle—signs, wonders and miracles—were done among you with great perseverance."*

There is another way to translate this verse that suggests that the signs of an apostle were worked in their midst and these signs were accompanied by patience and a display of the miraculous. This way of translating the verse is best exemplified in the *New English Bible* where it says, *"The marks of a true apostle were there, in the work that I did among you, which called for such constant fortitude, and was attended by signs, marvels and miracles."*

Earlier in Paul's writings he indicated that the proof of his apostleship was the existence of a church that he had founded. In other words, the work that he had produced was certification that he was in fact an apostle (see 1 Corinthians 9:2).

I remember hearing one apostolic ministry answer this question by saying that in the mother church that he had raised up, and the many outreach churches that had come forth from that mother church, miracles are commonplace. He may not be the one who does all of the miracles, but miracles are a part of the fruit of his life and apostolic ministry.

I think we need to believe God for a greater release of the supernatural in these days. The church of today is a long way off from where it was in the book of Acts, especially in this area of the supernatural. If they are going to see biblical results, apostolic ministries who help to break ground in new territories certainly need to be equipped with all of the spiritual tools that God has provided for them.

I think there are many *bona fide* apostolic ministries who do not have a strong ministry in signs and wonders. I am not going to reject them on this account. I am going to believe with them that the church of the twenty-first century is going to possess all of the gifts and graces of God so that it can be better equipped to fulfill the great commission.

5. *ALONG THIS SAME LINE, I HEARD ONCE THAT YOU HAD TO HAVE SEEN THE LORD IN PERSON TO QUALIFY AS AN APOSTLE. IS THIS TRUE?*

This teaching comes from Paul's comments in 1 Corinthians 9.1. Paul is defending his apostleship and says, *"Am I not an apostle? Am I not free? Have I not seen Jesus Christ our Lord? Are you not my work in the Lord?"*

Some feel that this indicates that an apostle must be one who has seen the Lord. Those who try to prove that apostles are not for today and were limited to the first century do so on the basis of this verse. They say that it confirms what is said in Acts 1 when the disciples were filling the place of Judas. One of the qualifications listed was to have been with Jesus.

Others feel that this is to be applied to current apostolic ministries. They suggest that since Paul's reference was most likely to his vision on the Damascus road, anyone who would be an apostle must have the same kind of encounter. This view promotes the idea that unless you have had Jesus personally come to you in a very dramatic fashion you do not qualify as an apostle.

I personally think this view is dangerous for a variety of reasons. First of all, it will again attempt to set the apostle apart from all of the other ministries of the body of Christ. It suggests that you must have a personal revelation of Jesus to be an apostle, but you do not need that same kind of visitation if you are going to be some other ministry.

Second, I think this view is dangerous because it bases a strict guideline on only one verse, and a fairly controversial verse at that. Again we must ask, "Is Paul using this statement to authenticate his apostleship?" If he is, do we have any evidence in the rest of the New Testament that Timothy, Barnabas, Epaphras or any other of those named apostles had this kind of experience?

In this same passage Paul asks another question where he says, *"Am I not free?"* If the issue of his seeing the Lord verifies his apostleship, in what way does his being free relate to his apostleship? Paul was evidently dealing with more than one issue in this verse.

I personally believe that every ministry needs to have seen the Lord. How do I mean that? I believe every ministry needs to have had some kind of encounter with the Lord whether it be through a vision, a dream, meditation on the Word of God, or a prophetic word. Every ministry needs to know that they have met God and they are doing what they are doing by His call and design.

6. *PAUL TALKS A GREAT DEAL ABOUT MONEY IN RELATION TO THIS MINISTRY. IT IS RIGHT FOR PEOPLE OR CHURCHES TO GIVE THEIR TITHE TO AN APOSTLE? HOW IS AN APOSTLE SUPPORTED FINANCIALLY?*

The issue of money did seem to be a big issue with Paul. On one hand, he continually affirmed his right, and the right of all ministries who labored in the Gospel, to live off of the Gospel. He continually affirmed the obligation of those who received spiritual ministry to give carnal things in return (see 1 Corinthians 9:11-14; Galatians 6:6). He continually supported the principle that the laborer is worthy of his wages (see 1 Timothy 5:17-18). Paul mentions specifically that as an apostle to the churches he had a right to financial support from those churches (see 1 Thessalonians 2:6).

On the other hand, Paul had many concerns in this area and knew of many abuses. For this reason, even though he defended the right of apostles to receive money for their ministry and implied that many others did so, he usually personally deferred that right.

Paul was perhaps too cautious in this area. He certainly had a right to be supported by the churches that he had established, but he continually refused to take money (see 1 Thessalonians 2:9). He actually worked very hard in his trade to finance his missionary journeys. Not only did he take care of his own expenses, he also covered the expenses of many who traveled with him (see Acts 20:33-34) When money ran low, he would open up a tent-making business until money was flowing again (see Acts 18:3).

When he was a prisoner in Rome, he had no choice. He was under house arrest and, while the Romans would allow him to live in his own hired house, they would not let him work in his tent-making business. While at Rome he accepted offerings from the churches to take care of his needs (see Philippians 4:10-20).

Paul saw himself as a real father to these new churches. He knew that they needed money themselves and he also knew the principle that parents are supposed to lay up for their children, not children for their parents (see 2 Corinthians 12:14-15). Paul said many times, *"I will not be burdensome to you"* (2 Corinthians 12:14).

Paul also did not want to be identified with what he referred to as false apostles who were only interested in the churches for what they could get out of them. He spoke of those who ministered for selfish ends and used flattering words to take big offerings (see 1 Thessalonians 2:5). Paul wanted to stay as far away from that spirit as he could.

Now back to the original question, we have already seen that it is all right for a church to voluntarily give money to the apostolic ministry over them. What about the tithe? What about the practice of tithing to a man or to a ministry?

I believe that when you touch the tithe you get into a whole different realm. There is no evidence in the New Testament that anyone tithed to a person. Some refer to Acts 4 when the people laid their offering at the feet of the apostles as an example. We must remember that at this stage in the development of the early church in Jerusalem, the apostles were the only eldership that this church had. This would be the equivalent of laying their offering at the feet of the elders of the church.

God makes it clear that the tithe is not something we are in control of. It is to go to the storehouse (see Malachi 3:10). It is to go to the place where God has recorded His name (see Deuteronomy 12:5,13-14). It is to go to the local church. If someone wants to give an offering beyond their tithe for some need that they see, they are free to do so; but the tithe belongs to the Lord.

The best way to avoid financial abuse is for apostolic ministries to be supported by the sending church. In church planting this is ideal because it allows the first salary to be given to the future pastor of the church. If all of the needs of the apostolic ministry are taken care of, it would immediately take money out of the decision-making process and free apostolic ministries from financial worry.

7. *I HAVE HEARD OF SITUATIONS WHERE A PERSON CALLING HIM-SELF AN APOSTLE HAS INVITED HIMSELF TO A CHURCH HE HAD NEVER VISITED TO GIVE A WORD OF CORRECTION OR ADJUSTMENT TO THAT CHURCH. IS THIS THE WAY APOSTOLIC MINISTRY WORKS?*

This is not the way that it is supposed to work. Unfortunately, there are many self-appointed apostles and prophets who travel around with no covering, accountability, or relationship. They think they are an apostle or prophet who can go into any church at any time with a word from the Lord.

Paul was an apostle. But even Paul realized that an apostle had to be sent by someone. He also realized that just because he was an apostle to one church, that did not automatically make him an apostle to another church or group. Apostolic ministry is a submitted ministry that is based on relationship.

If any ministry invited himself to my church or phoned me and said that God had given him a word for my church, red flags would go up. My first question to him would be, "To whom do you answer?" The second question would be, "To what local church do you belong?" Other questions would follow.

I would not accept this any more than I would accept a natural father coming into my house and talking to my children. He might say, "I am a father and I have a word for your family." I might say, "You might be a father, but I am their father! If you have a word for us, you can give it to me. If I feel it is good for them, I will share it with them."

8. *I HAVE HEARD OF SOME APOSTOLIC MINISTRIES THAT SEEM TO EXERCISE A LOT OF CONTROL OVER CHURCHES THAT ARE UNDER THEM—ALMOST TO THE POINT OF SMOTHERING THE LOCAL LEADERSHIP. WHAT DO YOU THINK ABOUT THIS? DOES THE BIBLE SHED ANY LIGHT ON THIS?*

Some people do seem to take their apostolic ministry too seriously. Raising up a church is a lot like raising a family. When the children are small, they need a lot of attention and supervision. But as they get older and respond to your teaching, you are able to give them more and more freedom until you are almost unnecessary. Hopefully, you will always have a good relationship with them and they will always have a desire for your counsel; but if you have done your job well, they will be able to make their own decisions most of the time.

When a church is just starting out it will often need plenty of close supervision. But as time goes by, the goal is for that church to be able to be autonomous—or self-governing, self-supporting, and self-propagating.

If apostolic leaders are not careful, they will smother the leaders that they are training. They want to keep them dependent (in the childhood stage) rather than letting them come to full adulthood. I have seen this happen to more than one apostolic church movement. The apostolic leader is strong and begins to train up pastors and church leaders who start churches. The apostle holds almost all of the power and must be in the middle of almost any decision of consequence. This works fine as long as the leaders are novices. However, as soon as the churches begin to grow and the pastors and local leaders get stronger themselves, they want their freedom.

These leaders want to control their own destiny. They want to follow their own dreams that have been placed in their hearts by the Holy Spirit. Inevitably, these types of situations end in crisis. Because the apostolic leader did not know when to let go, he can end up losing all of his spiritual sons and daughters.

How much control did Paul exercise over the churches that he established? Think about it for a minute. Paul did not have phones, FAX machines, e-mail, air travel, or any of the other modern means of communication that we have.

While he was physically at the places where he established churches, he most likely exercised a great deal of control. However, once his camel was out of sight down the dusty trail, he had no communication at all with them except through an occasional visit or letter.

When all is said and done, Paul only had a handful of contacts with any individual church once he had left them in the hands of the Holy Spirit. There was no day-to-day control. Paul could only speak to major doctrinal and practical issues. Paul had to trust that he had done a good job in teaching these leaders to hear the voice of Jesus—who is the Head of the church. He had to trust that the same Holy Spirit that was in him would be in them to guide them toward God's will.

9. *I AM A LITTLE CONFUSED BY WHAT YOU SAID REGARDING THE SENDING OF THE APOSTLE. IS THE APOSTLE SENT FROM GOD, FROM THE CONGREGATION OR FROM BOTH?*

An apostle is a sent one who must be called by God to function as an apostle. Without the calling of God and His provision of the needed gifts and graces for the call, the apostle has no authority to function in that ministry (see Romans 12:3).

However, it is just as important that the apostle be sent under the authority of the local church. Paul was an apostle from the point of his calling (see Acts 9:15-16; 26:16-18), but he was not released to function in that calling until it was recognized in the local church and hands were laid on him by the leadership of that church (see Acts 13:1-3). When they laid hands on him, they commissioned him as their representative in the field.

There are far too many ministries functioning outside of the local church today. The church is still the only institution ordained of God to fulfill the purposes of God in the earth (see Matthew 16:18; Ephesians 3:10-11). Every ministry, regardless of his or her specific calling, should be under the authority of a local church, fully submitted to its eldership and fully accountable to them in their ministry expression.

10. *WHAT IS THE APOSTLE'S RELATIONSHIP TO THE HOME CHURCH OR THE SENDING CONGREGATION?*

The apostle should be a fully functioning member of a local church just like every other person in the body of Christ. The apostle should be proven and approved for ministry in that setting and submit to the same spiritual qualifications given for elders (see 1 Timothy 3; Titus 1).

Any person who desires authority must first be under authority. The apostles in the New Testament were all related to the local church that was considered home. This was usually the sending body.

Once the apostle is sent out, however, the act of sending does not erase any ties or connections between the apostle and the sending church. The relationship should be strong and continue long into the future.

When Paul completed his missionary journeys, he always came home to report to the church and its leadership. While he was home, he plugged back into the everyday life and flow of the church, contributing his part to the success of the local church.

11. *TO WHAT EXTENT DO APOSTLES COVER THE CHURCHES AND THE MINISTRIES THAT THEY HAVE FOUNDED? ARE THEY INVOLVED IN THE DAY-TO-DAY OPERATIONS OF THE CHURCH? DOES THAT LESSEN AS THE CHURCH MATURES?*

The apostle provides fatherly care to churches and ministries much like parents do to their children. When they are young, the care is rather intense. As they get older, the parental involvement lessens until it is almost non-existent. At that point, even though the involvement is minimal, your father is still your father. The relationship goes on forever.

When a local church has its own eldership, it is covered by that eldership. When a church or ministry comes to adulthood, the apostle must be able to allow the Holy Spirit to faithfully lead and guide them into the future, much the same way that parents must release their married children into the purposes of God (see Acts 14:23; 20:32).

12. WILL EVERYONE HAVE AN APOSTOLIC RELATIONSHIP IN HIS OR HER LIFE? SHOULD THEY? WHAT DOES THAT LOOK LIKE IN PRACTI- CAL FUNCTION?

This is like asking, "Does everyone have parents?" In an ideal world, everyone has parents. But we do not live in an ideal world. There are orphans that exist in the world for a variety of reasons. Some children must grow up without the input of loving parents. Whether they have parents or not, they will grow up. You cannot stop the process.

The same is true in the spiritual realm. If the church were functioning the way God designed it, everyone would have spiritual fathers and mothers. Every church would have been started through the efforts of an Antioch church or one of its apostolic or leadership ministries. There would be a relational link in the life of every church and every church leader.

But for centuries the church has not been functioning the way God originally designed it. For this reason, ministries have been the product of their teaching—or lack of it. They have followed examples of ministers who have lived and fended for themselves. They have found themselves involved in church splits that had no resolution. They have, at times, had churches literally dropped in their laps with no one to turn to in their time of desperation.

It is hard to turn the clock back. It is hard to go back and build on a different foundation. It is hard to establish apostolic relationships after the fact. You will possibly never be able to experience the ideal. But, it is possible to gather together with others of like vision and enter into a covenant relationship with spiritual fathers and mothers and receive many of the blessings of apostolic relationships.

Today we see a movement among independent church leaders to come together into apostolic fellowships. C. Peter Wagner writes about this phenomenon in his book *The New*

Apostolic Churches. There is a hunger for relationship, not control. There is a desire for spiritual covering without sacrificing the autonomy of the church. God seems to be setting many solitary ones into families for the purpose of strengthening His church (see Psalm 68:6).

13. *HOW DO WE RECOGNIZE APOSTOLIC MINISTRY IN OUR LIVES?*

This is a little like asking, "How do I recognize my father." Your father is a natural relationship that you actually had no choice about. Some have fathers and some do not. Some have good fathers and some have bad fathers. Sometimes a father is no father at all. Sometimes people have been seriously abused by their father and for this reason have a negative view of fatherhood. In all of these situations there is a desire for fathers who genuinely love, really care, and who can be trusted to have our best interests at heart.

Usually, we can spot spiritual fathers and mothers because of a natural relationship. If we do not have that kind of relationship, we must look to those that God has placed near us and seem to genuinely love us, or are at least willing to be involved in our lives to some degree. Other times we might have to ask God to direct or lead us to those who have the same spiritual DNA (e.g. A grandfather, an uncle, or a cousin).

14. *I HAVE HEARD OF MINISTRIES HAVING A SPECIAL ORDINATION SERVICE WHERE THEY ARE ANOINTED WITH OIL AND SET ASIDE AS AN APOSTLE. IS THIS BIBLICAL? SHOULD ALL MINISTRIES HAVE SUCH AN ORDAINING SERVICE?*

First of all, it should be made clear that in the Old Testament, many ministries were anointed with oil at the time of their ordination. This was a symbolic act inspired by God to set aside or dedicate these ministries to the divine function. This practice is not specifically seen in the New Testament because in the New Testament, under the New Covenant, all believers are kings and priests to God.

Be that as it may, I do not think it is anti-biblical to anoint ministries, believers or even buildings. My only concern here is that we not let this practice be done for a singular ministry only. If we do this for apostles, why wouldn't we do this for all of the other ministries?

The main thing here is that we do not develop a practice in the church that elevates one ministry over another, thus establishing a spiritual hierarchy.

15. TO BE AN APOSTLE DO YOU HAVE TO BE RECOGNIZED BY OTHERS AS AN APOSTLE?

I think it would be great if Paul himself could answer this question, because we know that he was never fully received by some when it came to his apostolic ministry. God is vitally involved with every ministry that he has ordained. God, in His sovereignty, is the Head over all and is responsible for several things that relate to a person's ministry. God determines the kind of ministry that a person will have. He determines the sphere of influence that a person will have in ministry. He made Peter an apostle to the Jews and Paul an apostle to the Gentiles.

Not all apostles will be received as such by the entire body of Christ. Paul was not (see 1 Corinthians 9:1-2). It was not necessary for Paul to be recognized by all in order for him to function in his area of rule. Paul did know where he was received as an apostle and it was directly related to the places he had produced apostolic fruit. It is possible for a person to be considered an apostle to one group, but not be received as an apostle in another group.

The question remains, then, "Who should recognize an apostle?" An apostle should be recognized by as least four groups. First, an apostle should know it for himself. If you do not know you are called of the Lord, you will not likely convince anyone else.

Second, an apostle should be seen in that ministry capacity by the leadership in his own local church. This ministry should be proven in the local church and should be apparent to everyone that is close to him.

Third, the local congregation or the people in his home church should recognize an apostle. The members of the congregation are the ones who have witnessed his life among them. Do they bear witness to the call? Do they feel confident that the apostle is ready to represent them?

Finally, an apostle should be recognized by those he has grounded and established in the faith. Paul mentioned his apostleship in many letters, but he only defended his apostleship in the churches that he actually established. Apart from these four groups, the apostle needs no recognition except from God, the One the apostle is ultimately serving.

16. *THE BIBLE INDICATES THAT IN THE LAST DAYS THERE WILL BE FALSE APOSTLES AND FALSE PROPHETS. HOW CAN WE IDENTIFY AND GUARD AGAINST THESE MINISTRIES?*

Paul did warn against false apostles that will minister as angels of light among the churches (see 2 Corinthians 11:13-14). Paul seemed to indicate that there were a lot of ministries traveling with a wrong spirit from church to church in an attempt to impose their apostolic call on vulnerable churches and their leaders.

He compared his style and spirit with that of wrong apostolic style and spirit. Perhaps the best comparison is found in 1 Thessalonians 2:2-8. Here Paul gives the following comparison:

WRONG APOSTOLIC SPIRIT	RIGHT APOSTOLIC SPIRIT
Not:	*But*:
In error	In truth
In uncleanness	Blamelessly
In deceit	As a nursing mother
As men-pleasers	As God-pleasers
In flattering words	In gentleness
In covetousness	In love and affection
Seeking glory from men	As a father to his children
Demanding	Not burdensome

In the book of Revelation, Jesus commended the church at Ephesus for proving or testing apostles (see Revelation 2:2). As we approach the end times, this is something every church will have to become more aware of. Even Jesus taught that in the last days there would be false teachers, prophets, and apostles that would be very compelling in their teaching (see Matthew 7:15; 24:5,11,24; 2 Corinthians 11:13; 2 Peter 2:1; 1 Timothy 6:3-5; 2 Timothy 3:13).

False ministries prey on new converts (see Amos 6:4), the weak and immature (see 2 Peter 2:14), the gullible (see 2 Timothy 3:6), and the wounded and vulnerable (see Jeremiah 6:14). They are fueled by people who are discontented, unhappy, and weak in the faith.

False ministries are motivated by selfish ambition (see Philippians 1:16), covetousness (see Philippians 3:19), pride (see 1 Timothy 6:4), and the desire for a following (see Acts 20:30). They care more about themselves than they do the sheep (see Romans 16:18; Ezekiel 34:2-3,8). They speak smooth, persuasive, and flattering words (see Romans 16:18; Colossians 2:4).

The Bible says that you will know them by their fruit. The fruit of false ministries in the local church is bad. They cause division and strife (see Romans 16:17), are a source of constant friction (see 1 Timothy 6:4-5), unsettle souls (see Acts 15:24), scatter people (see Ezekiel 34:5-6), and do not profit the people of God (see Jeremiah 23:32).

Every leader has the potential to become a false ministry. To keep this from happening we must be willing to do five things:

1. *EXAMINE OUR OWN HEARTS.* Protecting ourselves means that we first examine the motives of our own hearts to see if we are in the ministry for all of the right reasons. Are we in the work of the Lord to make a name for ourselves? Do we like the idea of position and power? Are we ministering to fulfill a certain need in us? Are we motivated by personal financial gain?

    Examining our heart means a continual return to the heart of a servant. It is so easy to lose that heart as time goes on. Do we want to sit and be served, or do we want to serve. All ministers are first and foremost servants! Paul was a servant first and an apostle second (see Romans 1:1; 1 Corinthians 9:19).

2. *FOCUS ON THE BASICS.* Basic Christianity still works. We become vulnerable when we are constantly reaching out for the new or more exciting. As we focus on the basics of repentance, faith, love, fellowship, prayer, and the Word, we will stay on track.

3. *EXALT THE WORD.* The more people are taught the Word, the more ammunition they have against false teaching. We need to love the Word more than the miraculous. Signs are to confirm the Word, they do not replace it. We become vulnerable when we seek signs rather than letting signs follow. We need to be lovers of truth who preach the Word, teach the Word, meditate on the Word, search the Word, and, most of all, practice the Word.

4. *BE WILLING TO JUDGE AND SCREEN MINISTRIES.* I hate to say this, but we sometimes need to be a little skeptical (see Proverbs 14:15). Sometimes Christians are the most gullible people on earth. We want so much to believe and have a positive confession that at times we are taken in by false teaching.

   We need to become fruit inspectors. We do not just want to see short-term fruit, but long-term fruit. Having a big building, a TV ministry, and books in print are not the only things to look at. What fruit can be seen in the lives of those who follow?

5. *CULTIVATE FIRST LOVE.* Our greatest protection of all is having an up-to-date relationship with Jesus Christ. When we are dwelling in that place of first love relationship, Jesus Himself will help us to see through false ministries. The internal witness of the Holy Spirit must be trusted.

   This involves eliminating anything in our lives that may separate us from Jesus. As long as this relationship is in good order, we will have a firm foundation!

13

APOSTOLIC INTERVIEW

Dick Iverson is considered by many to be a present-day apostolic ministry. He began pastoring in the early 1950's with his parents and went on to raise up a true Antioch church in Portland, Oregon that has literally touched the nations of the world through its teaching, literature, tapes, and ministries.

Bible Temple (now City Bible Church), through his forty years of leadership, has become a model for many churches that seek to fill the apostolic role in the church world today.

Dick Iverson's apostolic fruit includes the founding of Portland Bible College in 1967, which has trained thousands of people for the call of God. Dozens of churches in North America and abroad have been birthed through ministries trained in this church. City Bible Church has also established a world-renown ministry team on the local level and a book-publishing ministry that is touching the world. Dick Iverson's fruit also includes the ongoing equipping of pastors and leaders through conferences and seminars.

In addition, in 1987, he established Ministers Fellowship International, a network of pastors and church leaders designed to strengthen ministries through relationship, accountability, and fathering care. In 1995, he made a successful transition out of the senior pastor role, passing the baton to one of his spiritual sons, Frank Damazio. He presently gives himself entirely to the nurture and care of the pastors and leaders who have become part of Ministers Fellowship International (MFI).

God has given Dick Iverson the true heart of a father and a very good understanding of what it means to be an apostle. For many years he resisted being called an apostle because of the abuse that he saw associated with it in the past. Many who called themselves apostles were using that title for their own enrichment. Now he is more comfortable when he is referred to in those terms.

Larry Asplund, one of the professors at Portland Bible College and an elder at City Bible Church, conducted the following interview with Dick Iverson, chairman of MFI.

LARRY ASPLUND: How would you define an apostle?

DICK IVERSON: I would think of an apostle as a person who has had extensive experience in the area of church building and ministry. An apostle couldn't be a novice for sure. Apostles are foundational ministries and if they haven't laid strong foundations in their own lives and ministries, whether it is establishing churches or pastoring churches, or raising up and pastoring leaders, they obviously wouldn't be in the season of life when I would think of them as an apostle.

I would also look at an apostle as having a ministry to "the ministry." He is fathering the fathers, and that would almost certainly require age. It would be hard to have some 25-year-old attempting to give input into a church or its eldership. There would have to be some longevity in his ministry, a proven track record that would give him the respect and credentials needed to function as an apostle.

I also think of an apostle as someone having a heart beyond his own immediate circle of fellowship. Many pastors of large churches are very concerned about their church only. I don't think they have an apostolic calling until they have a larger circle of burden and vision. Not only do they take care of their own, they also have a heart for other churches. They give their strength, not just to their own family, but also to other families. In other words, an apostle should be the kind of person who sows in another man's field and not just his own.

LARRY: How does a person become an apostle?

DICK: There are a lot of prophetic pronouncements being made today: You are an apostle. I had a young man in his twenties in my office this morning. He said that he was an apostle, and that when he goes back to his homeland, he expects they will receive him as an apostle. Well, that may happen in twenty years from now. But for him to go back and somehow expect to be a recognized apostle overnight...I personally don't think that will happen.

Sometimes that kind of expectation could actually damage a person. Any prophecy he may have received is futuristic anyway. If a prophet tried to fan that expectation too much, it could lead to a young person trying to do something he's not really qualified to do. I think the other danger is the view that you have to be seventy years old before you can be an apostle.

It is a gift that Jesus gave to the church. It is not something you personally choose. The call to the ministry of an apostle would maybe begin with the Lord putting a certain desire in your heart to want to work with other pastors.

It is a lot like being an apprentice carpenter. The apprentice gets around and just picks up the lumber for awhile. Pretty soon he pounds a few nails, and then he learns to do little more, and after a time he can build a house. You could have called him a "carpenter" at the beginning, but he really wasn't. That was his long-range destiny.

I don't see some magic wand that turns a person into an apostle. They develop into one because they have a gift in them that will emerge over time.

I've met pastors in their thirties that are apostolic in nature. By that I mean they are always thinking about the pastor down the street, how they can help him, how they can help his church through difficult times. They may not even have any connection with that church. They just have a heart for serving and helping the other guy.

LARRY: So, would you say that a person is to be recognized as an apostle because he has real relationships with people he is "apostling" and not just because he has some kind of word that he is one?

DICK: That's the key, Larry. I know of a couple of people who so badly want to be recognized as apostles. They're always in young leaders' faces, saying, "If I help you get started, you must recognize me as an apostle." Well, not everyone who helps you "get started" is a father to you. He might be a big brother.

I don't see how you can function as an apostle without you earning that level of respect, not by demanding it. You don't just say, "I'm an apostle, recognize me." Paul said, "I'm an apostle to some, and not to others." It's something people have to recognize in a leader, and when they recognize it, then the respect is there, they listen to their words, and they respond to their suggestions. It can't be forced on anybody.

Working with leaders is very interesting. Lots of people don't understand that leaders are very hard to work with. Because they are leaders they're very strong and have this instinct to go out ahead of others. So if you haven't earned their respect and if they don't trust you, if you haven't proven over the years that you love them and are there to serve them, they won't follow your "fatherly" advice just because you showed up.

LARRY: So, would you say apostolic ministry is really in some ways a certain kind of relationship?

DICK: That would be part of it. You know, if you talk to somebody who is wise and successful, you're going to try to extract some wisdom from them, whether or not you recognize him as an apostle in your life. That level of relationship exists simply out of respect for who a person is and what he has accomplished.

Then you have the next level of relationship, a father-son relationship. This level of relationship is not just for information. You are now "walking together in the Gospel." As a father to a son, you want him to succeed, and as he succeeds, it is like your son succeeding. His success is your reward, that's your paycheck, that's what makes you rejoice.

LARRY: So, would you say apostolic authority functions voluntarily?

DICK: Absolutely! Absolutely! And I think this is where many are getting in as they believe for the restoration of true apostolic ministry.

Some people teach that the apostle is at the top of the totem pole. He's worked his way up, and now he's just another Pope over certain churches. That's very dangerous. That's not the way even Paul operated. He did not have the ultimate authority in the churches he related to. If anybody should have, he should have. But he reminded the church at Corinth that he did not have dominion over their faith, but he was a helper for their joy (see 2 Corinthians 1:24). To me, that is the spirit of an apostle. "I'm not taking dominion over your life, I'm a helper."

Some people see an apostle as being so dominant that when they walk into a church, the resident eldership just sits down and makes all the course adjustments the apostle requires of them. And then when the apostle walks out, he hands the reins of the church back to the leadership of that church. That's not only unbiblical, it is very dangerous. This idea of trans-local authority makes me very nervous.

LARRY: Especially if it is functioning in a hierarchical chain of command rather than relationally?

DICK: That's right! Exactly! Everything in God's kingdom has to do with relationships. We relate to God, we relate to the Holy Spirit, we relate to each other. You know, it's about family. Everything is relational. It's in the spirit realm, in the natural – everything is about relationships.

So whenever you try to define an apostolic relationship in terms of a hierarchy, things will break down very fast. It's hard to respond to people because you have to. It's like the way we function in our minister's fellowship, we don't want people to be members of the fellowship if they don't have or want relationship. We don't own people or control their lives, but we do relate to people.

LARRY: What was your first experience with apostolic ministry?

DICK: I was 32 when I became the senior pastor of our congregation. I did not have real pastoral training. I was an evangelist and had served as a co-pastor with my dad. The main responsibility for the church had been on his shoulders for the first 10 years of the church. So when I had to take the primary leadership role, I began to look for models I could learn from. I had to ask myself what kind of church I wanted to build. Then I needed to find someone who was building that kind of church.

I found that person in Reg Layzell of Vancouver, B.C., Canada. When I visited Glad Tidings in Vancouver, I saw a church that was extremely strong in worship, extremely strong in prayer, and strong in unity. And I told myself, "I want a church like that." I did not know what it would take to get there, I did not understand the theological foundation of it, I just knew the spirit of that church. I knew it was the kind of church I would like, and the kind I did not have. I had no worship, no prayer and no unity. And those were the three things I saw in Reg Layzell's church.

So, he earned my respect immediately by what he had produced. If you don't like what the guy is producing, you might like him, but you're not going to give yourself to eating out of his bucket.

Reg Layzell was a very straight, some people would say hard, man. What he believed, he believed, and there was no bending him. I mean it was, "That's the way it is, and if you don't do it that way it's absolutely wrong." Reg Layzell was that type of a leader. I think he was a true apostle.

He established a number of churches after establishing a great "mother" church. He was very mission minded and provided many countries with godly men that we still walk with today.

But he also respected the local resident pastors. I remember the first time he came to visit us here. It was 1965, when our church really exploded. Like a flower, it just came into full bloom almost overnight, although preparation had been going on for a number of years. Suddenly, the presence of God just came down upon us. The worship ascended and the people united in prayer.

I remember one of the first services with Brother Layzell. We were in a dynamic flowing service. I was the novice in that context, but I was in charge. David Schoch, a proven prophet, was sitting next to me. Reg Layzell, the apostle, was sitting on the other side of me. I had a very high regard and respect for both of them.

The service was just exploding with the presence of God. There was a strong prophetic anointing and a strong flow of worship. The river was just flowing, and I was blessed. But I also did not know what to do with it. I had no idea how to handle this kind of service. You don't want to put your hand on the power of God, so I was scared to death that I would mess up the river.

I just stood there, and as the service began to kind of "wind down" I turned to Reg Layzell and I said, "Brother Layzell, do you want to take the service?" And he looked at me with a scowl on his face, and he grunted, "Huh, I'm not the pastor here." And he wouldn't take the service. I did not know what to do, but he wouldn't let me stand back and not take the lead. I wanted him to take the service, but he forced me to the front, which was the right thing to do. He was right there, and if I would have "goofed up" he would have helped me. But he made me jump in and start swimming in the river. He made me take charge and do what I was supposed to do.

I was in a real learning mode during that season of my life. Anything he would have said, that's the way it was going to be. He marked my life permanently with certain key principles.

For example, in 1965 we were a very small church with a small income. In fact, I was working on the side. So money was an issue. We had flown both of the brethren in for services. Although we had a wonderful time, they couldn't give me a Sunday, so I did not have the Sunday offering to help with the expenses.

I'd had a lot of evangelists in before this. A lot of these guys were there for the money. They wanted to live high even though money was hard. I was often disillusioned with these evangelists. So, when I went to give Brother Layzell an honorarium after he had ministered, I handed him a check for $250.00 for three nights in the middle of the week. That would probably be equivalent to at least $1000.00 today. I wanted to stretch to give him as much as I could because he had blessed us so much. I had given money like this to other evangelists who were well known, and they sometimes snarled at me, "Is that the best I'm going to get out of this, is that all you're going to give me?" So, I purposely put the check in an envelope and licked it shut so I wouldn't have to see his disappointment.

I was in my office and said, "Here, Brother Layzell, here's your honorarium." He slowly got out his glasses, and I thought, "Oh no." He opened the envelope and looked at the $250.00 check. He let out a grunt, threw it on the desk and said, "Nope, nobody is worth this kind of money."

Then he lectured me. "You start paying this much and you'll get all the flakes in the country around here. You don't want people coming here because of money, you want them coming because they are going to build your church."

LARRY: Obviously, your relationship with Brother Layzell was voluntary. Nothing was forcing you to submit to him.

DICK: Nothing was forcing either of us. In fact, we differed on several areas of doctrine. Actually, we were not on the same page at all in some doctrinal areas. But I was on the same page with him when it came to building a good church.

LARRY: How did you decide to respond to him, to relate to him and receive him?

DICK: I respected him personally. We simply did not get into areas where we differed. We agreed on praise and worship, we agreed on prayer, we agreed on the unity of the local church, the importance of the local church, and those were the areas I would always have him preach on when he came. I had him preach the kind of church both he and I wanted. I saw him as a father. He was a straight shooter, a man of integrity. He had a great vision for missions. And so he rubbed off on me in a lot of areas. But not because he forced his ideas on me. It was because of my respect for him.

LARRY: And you did not feel the need to agree with him on every point?

DICK: Oh no! And he did not try to force me, either. We would talk about a lot of things, but he never forced his ideas on me. In fact, he later admitted he had been wrong in some areas in which we differed.

LARRY: How would you say your relationship over the years with Brother Layzell benefited you and the church?

DICK: Well, I "fed out of his bucket" for years and years. I would go up to Vancouver once or twice a year, even if I did not preach (which I didn't very often) and just observed, watched and listened.

I observed the prayer room and established it at my church at home. I remember when we first started the prayer room, the women were on one side and the men on the other so it would be modest. I did everything just the way he did it. I directed our services like he did. I took a hard line on the distinctives I had learned from him. We had strong prayer, strong worship, and strong unity.

He was the apostle of praise, for sure. That was the mark of the church. That was a key because that has to do with the presence of God, God releasing the power of his presence. And it was great.

But he was a no-nonsense guy. If an evangelist came around that was a flake, he let everybody know it.

LARRY: You weren't necessarily buddies with him? You did not vacation with him?

DICK: No! No! I was not that close. We were good friends, I respected him highly, but no, we were never that close. He was maybe 25 years older that I. He had different personal interests. I was raising my children at the time. If he had asked me to I would have happily gone with him anywhere. But, no, we weren't that close.

But I was that close in the Spirit to him. I've found through life that most of your mentoring is not necessarily done fishing, but is the example of your life. If people really want to know what you know, let them get next to you and once they do, things will become "more caught then taught."

LARRY: Apostolic ministry is authority as well as relationship. But his authority in your life existed because you welcomed it.

DICK: I was always sucking him dry, getting everything I could out of him, always asking questions. But, again, he did not demand that I agree with him. He told me what he believed and then it was up to me to sort it all out.

LARRY: So, how does it work in your experience today? We need living models in the church today. It can be very difficult for us to imagine true apostolic ministry. We have the denominational model, and then we have the radically independent church model, and very little in between. Could you describe how apostolic relationships work for you today?

DICK: That is the key question, "How do you relate to some and not to others?" When I go into certain places, I feel a certain pulling on me to help. In other places I don't feel any pull at all. I'm just the speaker. Some sit down and say, "I want you to be an apostle to this church." I ask them, "What do you expect from me if I am to be an apostle to you?" Some then tell me, "That you be available, that I can call you, that I can talk to you, that you will come periodically."

I have to be real careful that I don't get their expectations too high or then they get disillusioned. "You said you were going to come here every month, and you don't. You only see me a couple times a year." So, I have to be careful when they ask for an apostolic relationship. I want to be honest with them. There are only 52 weeks in a year so there are only 52 churches I can visit a year.

Our fellowship has several hundred pastors in it. Obviously, I cannot be in every church very much. I believe in the philosophy, "If you cannot go to the mountain, get the mountain to come to you." That's why we have annual conferences and regional conferences in our fellowship of pastors. At least there are a few days we can mingle together. There's a lot of apostolic work that goes on during a conference.

Then there are a lot of phone calls that come in. Some don't want much from me. They just want to feel that they have a safety valve if anything goes wrong. I may rarely even talk to them. They just need a kind of insurance policy. They need to have an apostolic minister that can respond and help when they feel the need.

There are really many levels of apostolic relationship. I may never preach in a pastor's church, and yet he feels very close to me, and I to him, as friends. He may call me once a year to talk over a problem. Then there are other guys who get into certain seasons when they feel the need to talk to me every week. If they're walking through some difficult times I try to meet their need.

So, I don't think there is stereotype, a certain way that an apostle must function. It depends on the situation, the need, and the desire for relationship.

It is even affected by geography. We have people around the world that look to us. They may be 10,000 miles away, but we still maintain communication with them. Now with e-mail and the fax machine, communication is much easier. When leaders get into trouble, we get an e-mail from them with questions.

It's similar to pastoring a church. If you pastor a church of 500 people, you have a lot of problems. If you have 500 ministers looking to you, there will be a lot of problems. Paul said that he felt the pressure of his concern for the churches every day (see 2 Corinthians 11:28). I can understand that now. If you give the wrong counsel, you can destroy a church. If you don't give them any counsel you can destroy a church. So, you feel the needs out there. It humbles you and you find yourself praying, "God help me now. Help me to be able to help them through this situation, and not to give them wrong advice."

I've watched apostolic ministries ruin churches. So I walk in fear and trembling. I would rather not even get involved in a situation unless it is clearly the leading of the Lord for me to do so. In other words, I'm not looking for authority or responsibility. It has to come to me. I have such a great respect for the pastor and leadership team in the local church. I just want to help them. I don't want to be a burden to them.

LARRY: I'm sure you have been called into problem situations in local churches. How did that work?

DICK: There are two ways I might be called. One is, the senior pastor can call me in. In my experience 95%, and maybe higher, of local church problems are in leadership. It's like in a family. When husband and wife are fighting, that's where the real problem is. When the kids are acting up, if Mom and Dad are in unity, they can generally handle it. It's the same with the local church, if there are problems in the congregation, we usually don't get too involved. But when leadership is involved, it's much more dangerous. There's often a split, a division, and a real struggle. In such cases, the senior pastor can invite us in to help.

Or, in the second case, the elders can invite us in. Maybe the senior pastor is the problem. In either case, both the senior pastor and the elders must have agreed in advance they will call us in if there's an emergency or a need for some kind of assistance.

LARRY: So, if the elders as a group, not counting the senior pastor, called you on the phone and asked you to come, you would come?

DICK: Yes. But first, I would call the pastor up and say, "I've been asked by your eldership to come in and talk over some things that are concerning them. Would you be in agreement with and confirm their request?"

LARRY: It would have to be a very serious issue, not just, "We're not getting along?"

DICK: No, I wouldn't come in if they were just bumping each other, although even in that situation a voice from the outside can help both parties to gain perspective. Normally, it would be something more serious having to do with moral issues, financial mismanagement, or some charge that could actually disqualify them as an elder before I would get involved. Even then it can be very tricky. Let me give you an example.

There's one church I'm thinking of that was under the influence of another apostle. The senior pastor had been convinced by one of the elders that he had disqualified himself from leadership in the church. They called in their apostolic father who agreed with the elder's accusation. And so, they convinced the senior pastor to resign. He had been there for sixteen years. They were in the middle of a multimillion-dollar building program. They had a congregation of nearly eight hundred people. And they convinced him that he should resign. So he publicly resigned.

After he resigned, he had second thoughts. "I shouldn't have resigned. I haven't done anything wrong." So he called me and said, "Brother Dick, I need somebody to come and listen to what is going on here. I have resigned, but I think it was a major mistake. Would you come?" I had no apostolic relationship with this church, although I was a friend of their apostolic father. So I said, "The only way I will come is if this other apostolic brother asks me to."

Well, it so happened that the other brother called me and proposed that we both go down and meet with the elders. So, I went down there and met on a Monday night. The elder that had first brought an accusation against the pastor walked in with a manila folder about two inches thick full of charges. With that amount of evidence I was expecting to find out that the Pastor been caught in a motel with his secretary or something equally serious. Instead, the charges were that he had been heard laughing behind closed doors with his secretary. And just a lot of things like that. I kept waiting for something, but there was nothing of substance. It was just a lynch mob. The accusing elder was what I would call an "Absalom."

So, I talked with the other apostle and said, "You know, you are going to split this church and cause it to go into bankruptcy, and there is no grounds for it. The pastor may need counsel or minor adjustment, but he does not need dismissal."

My friend said, "What would you do?" I said, "I would have the pastor go back to the people with your support, and tell them his resignation had been a mistake, that there had been no immorality whatsoever, and that he and his family would be submitting to counsel. Tell them he is going on a sabbatical for 60 to 90 days, and then he'll be back." He agreed, and I know it saved that church.

My friend denied that the other elder was an Absalom, but two weeks later he came in to the pastor's office and said, "I'm going across town and starting another church." So, he was an Absalom, and he did take a couple hundred people out of the church and leave. He's down to about sixty now. He's not going to make it, because he's building on the wrong foundation.

That's the real joy of my ministry, to see a church rescued and saved. Today, that congregation and leadership team is back up to full steam. They've finished their building, the pastor is doing great, he and his wife are happier than ever. Seeing that is my reward. Once in awhile we win one. Unfortunately, we occasionally lose them too.

LARRY: I'm interested in your own personal story. I know you didn't wake up some morning, and say, "My goodness, I'm an apostle." But, you have had a process that you've gone through in your own ministry and in your relationships. How did that happen?

DICK: My wife and I spent 14 years, 10 under my father and 4 under my leadership, with 100 people. Win one, then lose one. We recycled people for 14 years. I went through all kinds of extremes.

At first we were called Deliverance Temple, with an emphasis on healing ministry. During that time, I did not like pastoring at all. I wanted to quit. Having a business was better. I enjoyed being an evangelist where I could just keep moving and was always the hero.

I think I went through about everything you could go through during those years. And so, when I see some of the things a pastor might be going through today, I can say, "I was there." I know exactly where he's going, and I know that if he does not change certain things he will pay a price for it. Like the Bible says, we can comfort those who are in trouble with the comfort we have received (see 2 Corinthians 1:4). I feel for them.

Recently I was in a church that was about to split. I could see each side very easily, because I've been on both sides. And I was able to help them.

But no, you don't find "Apostle" written in large letters on my door. I would rather say that I do apostolic work. It isn't just a title, it's work, W-O-R-K.

Apostolic ministry is processed over time. It is like the CEO who was asked what the key to his success was. He said, "Good decisions." And then he was asked how you make good decisions. "Experience." How do you get experience? "Bad decisions."

That has been my process. I'm not smart enough to learn out of books. I've got to get out there and get bumped around and learn the hard way. "The stove's hot, you don't touch that stove."

As a church, we began to learn important apostolic princi ples from Reg Layzell. And then God began to bless us, and we started seeing growth come. Then we started Portland Bible College and began to train leaders. To whom much is given, much is required. I just felt we needed to give away our bread. Then we started the Northwest Ministers Conference to help pastors and leaders who were hungry.

Then we started planting churches. In a sense, we were forced into working with leaders. And the day came when I was wearing two hats: trying to pastor this work and trying to help others leaders. I had become more than a pastor. I had become a father.

LARRY: When you began planting churches how did that affect your responsibilities?

DICK: That was what really forced the issue. The first church we planted was in Troutdale. It did not make it. And then we went to Hood River and planted a second church that eventually did make it. We weren't batting very well to start with, but we were sure learning.

And then we probably averaged 3 church plants a year for awhile. Instead of just sending a couple out to start a church, we sent teams of 20, 30, up to 50 people. This way the new pastor actually began with an embryo church, and as a result it usually grew quite quickly. Taking care of these church plants and their pastor is really what brought my ministry to where it is today.

LARRY: Did you have a formal relationship with the leaders you sent out?

DICK: It was much more informal then than it is now. In those days I would probably say, "Well, you're OK, you don't need me. I'm going to go out and help somebody else who is obviously struggling and bleeding." Eventually, my own sons said, "Hey, you don't have time for us. You're always out helping everybody else. How about your own sons?" And I realized I did have responsibility to my own sons.

Now we have a more formal relationship. By having a systematic, structured fellowship, I know I will see everybody at least twice a year. And maybe more. Before I might have had a church plant, but I was so busy trying to help everybody else out that two or three years could have gone by without me even visiting their church, let alone spending a few days in a conference with them.

Our present relationship has brought great relief to me. I know that we're going to spend 3 or 4 days together on a regular basis. Sure, it will be at a regional or annual conference, but still, we'll be there. I can't take care of every situation that may come my way. It is necessary to have a structured, developed ministry relationship. Fortunately, I now have others working with me who can minister apostolically as well.

LARRY: Did your books contribute to your growing influence?

DICK: At first, all of our books were written for our own use. And then people said, "Can we have them, too?" So, the books were the way the lessons and principles we had learned here began to spread.

LARRY: Does the nature of your apostolic relationships with other leaders grow and change over time?

DICK: Absolutely! In the case of a new church plant, I make more of an effort to speak into that church in its embryo stage. But then as the church grows, the nature of our relationship changes.

It's kind of like raising a child. A day will come when your young adult will look you straight in the eye and know that he knows as much about some things as you do. You'll still have his respect, but he doesn't need you now in the same way he did when he was a baby. He doesn't need your constant coddling, "Don't do this, son, don't do that." He grows, he matures, and so our relationship moves to a different, more of an equal basis.

That's no threat to me personally. I'm thrilled to walk into a church that was once fragile and struggling for survival and now is a powerful, strong church. That church does not really need me to be a father to them. They may need me to be a friend, and as an insurance policy in case they get in trouble. What I want to avoid is what I've seen several of my friends get into. They never let their sons grow up. They kept the lid on the decision process. "We'll tell you what to teach, what to preach, how to act, what not to do, what to do." That may be acceptable when you're little and you're trying to learn how to walk. But once a son has his own children, his own family, then it is abnormal for someone to come in and tell them how to raise their family.

I've seen several church fellowships where the apostle wanted to keep a heavy hand on everything and everybody. I don't know if it's insecurity or what. My approach would be to be more hands-on when they're young and they could hurt themselves unnecessarily, but as soon as you can, to back off and give them room to be themselves, to have their own personality.

In our fellowship, we have a lot of people with different ministry styles and emphases. They're all great people. They all love God, but they lead a little differently from the way I might do it. And hey, that's beautiful. I can't fault them. We don't want just a bunch of sausages forced into my mold. They all have their own personalities. But wha's more important, they do share our church principles and core distinctives. They just may express them a little differently.

14

INTERVIEW CONTINUED

LARRY ASPLUND: The name of the apostolic fellowship you give leadership to is Ministers Fellowship International. How did MFI get started?

DICK IVERSON: Our fellowship began when Bible Temple (now City Bible Church) started to systematically train leaders. We started a Bible College, Portland Bible College, in 1967. Soon we had a growing number of Bible College graduates, and since we are a nondenominational church, there was no place to send them to "try out." So, over the course of time, we built up a number of qualified leaders that were working in the church, but who really had a call to pastor and establish churches of their own.

In the mid-70's we began to plant churches. We would send out a small group of people to the location for which they had a burden. We made sure they were equipped and trained. They would be identified in the congregation as someone we had approved to plant a church in a certain city. Those who wanted to be a part of the church planting team had to communicate their desire to their district pastor and be screened first. Then they could begin meeting with the church planter. It usually would take six months to a year for the entire process.

During this time, we had a church within a church, a kind of embryo church in the womb. When the time came, the elders prayed over them, gave them some help financially, and sent them out to their city. We started a number of churches this way, and still follow the same basic procedures today.

Bible Temple (City Bible Church) was a mother church to a network of churches that we had planted. So, we had a special responsibility for them since they were our spiritual sons and daughters. We had trained them and sent out.

In order to assist in our follow-up of these planting pastors, we began to bring all of them together once a year to meet as "Bible Temple outreach churches." Those in attendance were limited to only those churches that we had officially planted and for which we were personally responsible.

At the same time, God was continuing to bless Bible Temple. We were healthy and growing. So, over time, we became a kind of watering hole for pastors of diverse backgrounds. These were not pastors whom we had sent out and we had no direct responsibility for them. Nevertheless they wanted to "eat from our bucket." As a result, as early as 1976, we began offering the annual Northwest Ministers Conference. Pastors from all over the area, and eventually all over the world, would gather in May. In addition, the Bible Temple outreach churches had an annual meeting in November.

The May meeting was quite large because it was an open conference. One of the recurrent themes that would come up in our relationship and dialogue with many of these pastors was covenant relationships and that everyone should be accountable and should not be independent in spirit. Little by little, the inevitable happened. Pastors who had no sending church or apostolic ministries in their life started coming to us and saying, "Can we be part of your outreach churches and identify with you?" But we really had no process or structure for what they were talking about and so there was really no place for them.

To be an outreach church they would have to come to our church, go to school, and be sent out from us to be an outreach church. Of course, that was totally impractical because these were churches that were already existing, established, and self-governing that wanted to have some kind of relationship with us.

After a while, I began to feel like we were talking out of both sides of our mouth. On the one hand, we were telling them they needed relationship and covering; but on the other hand we were refusing to relate to them in that way. Over the course of time, the pressure continued to mount to do something about it. I was resisting because I knew the cost to me personally and the outreach church pastors were resisting because they did not want to share their piece of the pie with so many others. We had never wanted to have large numbers of people. We were just trying to take care of our own. Some of the outreach church pastors were very comfortable with the way things were. The concept was "us four and no more" and we want Dad's total attention.

When I eventually brought up the idea of opening our fellowship to pastors of churches that we had not directly planted, not everyone was very enthusiastic about doing it. But they weren't the ones taking the heat. I was the one those pastors were approaching. We never wanted to have worldwide fellowship, we just wanted to take care of those God had placed in our path.

Finally, in the early 80's, the thing that forced us to reconsider the scope of our fellowship was the case of a small fellowship of pastors that had disintegrated. Their leader, their spiritual father, had "blown it" and was now out of the picture. Two of those young pastors, probably in their upper twenties, called me on the phone within few days of each other. "We don't have any spiritual covering now. Can we come and be part of the Bible Temple outreach churches?" There were no procedures so I said, "Look, I'll help you. You come to the Northwest Ministers Conference and we'll help you. In the meantime, you call me if you need anything."

I knew at the time that's not what they wanted. They wanted to be part of the family. They wanted real relationship. But I stiff-armed them, kindly, and told them we'd help them the best we could. Within a month, both of them had shipwrecked their homes and separated from their wives. They had pleaded with me to help them, and I had turned them down. I realized that when they were on the phone to me, they were already in trouble. The Lord took me to the woodshed over that.

So, I went back to our outreach church pastors, (around 30 of them at the time) and told them, "I don't care what we have to do, I don't care what procedures we adopt, there must be a way we can have real relationship with leaders who want to walk with us." By this time there was a consensus in the group. As a result, we started the process of broadening our relationships. We did not want a denomination. We did not want to establish a hierarchy of control. We did not want to own church property. We just wanted relationship.

We discussed criteria for an extended fellowship to pastors. We felt that those who would be a part had to be without a spiritual family, therefore, they could not be a part of some other organization or denomination. We must have a clear, personal relationship with them. We had to know them, to have been to their church. They had to have demonstrated integrity of character. They had to be people who we could trust and believe in. Doctrinal compatibility was also very important. How could we walk together if we could not agree? This did not mean that there had to be total agreement on every single point of doctrine, but there certainly had to be compatibility on the essentials. When we minister in one another's churches, we don't want to have to clean up the mess when it is over.

The four pillars that we felt had to serve as a foundation to our coming together were covenant relationship, integrity of character, commonality of vision, and doctrinal compatibility. I know it is true that almost all denominations started as a fellowship and then later evolved into something other than that. We, in fact, wanted to offer most of the things that would typically be found in a denomination. But we somehow wanted to protect ourselves from going in the traditional direction of control. We wanted to protect the autonomy of the local church. As a result, we built in some additional things that would decrease the chances of our going in the typical direction.

We insisted on limiting four areas of function in relation to the fellowship. We determined that we would not hold any church properties, we would not form a central Bible school, we would not form a central missions board, and we would not license or ordain ministries. All of these things, we felt, are the function of the local church and all of these things are the things that lead to control over local churches and their pastors.

This does not mean that we would not be a resource to pastors and counsel in relation to any of these areas. It simply means that we would not have any controlling voice in these local church decisions. We would encourage a voluntary cooperation between our member pastors when it comes to missions and the like, but we don't want to control their activities or collect their mission money.

We then discussed how we should govern ourselves as a fellowship. We realized we needed a team of leaders. Just like a local church has an eldership, we needed an eldership over the fellowship. So, we formed an "Apostolic Leadership Team." I serve as the Chairman, Frank Damazio serves as Vice Chairman and we have about twenty others who serve on the team with us.

The members of this team are not all apostles per se. Some are prophets, some are strong pastors of apostolic churches, but they all have one thing in common—a father's heart. They're interested in more than just their own church. We selected a group of leaders who had proven their ministry and leadership among us. They were individuals that I had walked with in fellowship for years. This group, the Apostolic Leadership Team, serves as the directors of the fellowship.

As time has gone on, we also developed regional leaders. We now have eleven regions in the United States. Each region has a regional director, who is also a member of the Apostolic Leadership Team. When we get together, we have representatives of the entire nation. In this way, we can become more aware of the activities and the needs in every part of the nation.

We meet twice a year for several days to discuss the needs of the fellowship as well as current issues that pastors and churches are facing. We also deal with financial and administrative matters relating to the operation of the fellowship.

You cannot have an effective, working organization without finances. We decided to ask for membership dues on a sliding scale. The little church pays just a relatively small amount, and the larger churches pay more. We try to keep the dues as small as possible so as not to be a burden to the members and yet still be able to fulfill the express purposes of the fellowship.

In 1995, I stepped away from my responsibilities as a senior pastor so I could give full time to MFI. I have a number of very capable leaders who assist me in the office, including Bill Scheidler, our administrator. We provide day-to-day oversight of the needs of the fellowship.

We don't attempt to provide oversight to any local church. We have a very strong conviction that the local church is to be self-governing, self-supporting and self-propagating. We do not adhere to most of the concepts of trans-local authority (i.e. some authority outside of the local church attempting to control the local church). We come to a church by invitation only and when we do, we come in functioning under the eldership or the authority of the house.

Obviously, if I knew a pastor was in trouble, I would call him. But, if there was some major problem they wanted help with, either the senior pastor could call us in, or the elders as a group could call us in—by invitation only.

There is a specific process by which a minister may become a member of MFI. You must begin your process with a "sponsor." The sponsor is a senior pastor or member of the Apostolic Leadership Team who is already a member and is a key person who represents the first level of relationship. The sponsor is really the key to participation in the fellowship.

Let's say you have a church and have joined MFI through sponsorship. Later you may have six church plants. You then might sponsor each one of those six into the broader fellowship, but that would not take away your responsibility to maintain your fatherly care over the churches that you have established.

You see, we are not trying to break any relationships that already exist. If anything, we want to fan them. In fact, if one of those six churches would call me personally and say, "Brother Dick, would you come and help us?" The first thing I would ask is, "Who is your sponsor?" If their sponsor wants me to step in, he can ask me himself. In this way, we maintain proper covering on all levels.

In our fellowship, there are several clusters of local churches that continue to look to a spiritual father or mother church. All roads don't lead to Rome. Indirectly, they could come and get help from me, but I want them to look to their covering church first, and then to MFI. Our fellowship is like an umbrella. We have a larger fellowship that pastors and church leaders can draw ministry from, but they're still committed to the person and church that sent them out.

A lot of people still have a denominational "headquarters" mentality. They forget that it is all about relationships.

LARRY: How does the regional director function?

DICK: A regional director works with his team to be a resource for a group of leaders in a geographical area. They are in regular contact with the MFI members in their assigned area. All the

members of the regional leadership team are pastors themselves. Each member of the team might be in contact with five
or more churches. It is a smaller network within the fellowship.

If the regional director has a difficult problem with which
he wants help, he can call me, or anybody else he feels could
help him. But we still would work hard to not sever any existing
relationships. We really work hard, Larry, to not pull you away
from your spiritual father or other established relationships.

We know that there are many groups like ours that are trying to accomplish the same thing that we are. We certainly do
not think we are the only group that is meeting an important
need among pastors and church leaders. We're just one of the
"tribes in Israel." And we're not any better than any other tribe.
There's one church, one kingdom, but many tribes. Each one
has its own distinctives and emphases. It does not mean we
have it all, or we're better in any way.

We believe in what we're doing or we wouldn't do it. We're
not in competition with anyone else and we don't feel that if
you're not in MFI you're somehow "missing out." In fact, we
have no growth goals. God seems to have led certain ones to us
and we want to be faithful to do what God has called us to do.

LARRY: And now you have begun to expand internationally.
How are these new fellowships developing?

DICK: Many of the international fellowships are the result of
years of missionary work. A long-term missionary has become a
catalyst in a nation to help other pastors. Or perhaps we have
gone over to certain countries to minister down through the
years and have a relationship with many of the pastors and leaders in those countries. We don't just pick a nation and start a fellowship. There has to have been a prior relationship with them.

For some time we have had international pastors as members of MFI, but they have a long way to travel to attend any of

our conferences. We give them the "Seed Bag" four times a year, which contains good material, but there still is not the same quality of relational connection that we're looking for. It's extremely difficult for a pastor from a third world country, or from any country for that matter, to maintain a consistent relationship with us. The cost of travel and maintaining their dues is often beyond their reach.

Because of this fact, we felt very strong that we needed to do something in nations where we were relating to a number of pastors. We wanted to try forming a leadership team in those nations and help them make their own apostolic connections and form an affiliated fellowship within their own geographical region.

We started in Australia with Kevin Conner. That was easy to do because Kevin was with us here in Portland for ten years and has walked very closely with us. Now Ministers Fellowship of Australia has formed with Kevin as the chairman. We get together periodically with him for relationship but MFA is totally self-governing. They do function with all of the same principles and overall guidelines that we do in MFI.

LARRY: Is Kevin Conner a member of your Apostolic Team?

DICK: Yes, he's a member. Our goal is that the chairman of every international, affiliated fellowship be a part of one apostolic leadership team.

For instance, there are several good pastors in West Africa who have had a lot of interaction with some of our people. So we're forming a leadership team there to coordinate a Ministers Fellowship of West Africa. The same is true in Europe and Brazil and Mexico and East Africa. In every case, we know and relate to the key people who make up the Apostolic Leadership Teams in those countries.

LARRY: Let's talk than about the annual conference and the Seed Bag, and some of the other things you do to feed the pastors.

DICK: The most important thing is RELATIONSHIP in capital letters. Everything we do is designed to expedite relationships. The Seed Bag is a very interesting concept. We didn't want to just have the typical periodical with articles and other promotional materials. We wanted to put tools into the pastor's hands that would assist and further equip leaders. We wanted to give the pastor tangible resources that would help to strengthen them and their churches.

We came up with the concept of the Seed Bag. Four times a year we send out a package that contains two or three books and three or four teaching tapes, all on a leadership level. We try to provide cutting edge leadership material, the most current books, the things that are really hot. Four times a year we send articles, information, directories, activity ideas, biographies, books and tapes. It is a nice size package.

In addition to the Seed Bag, we have regional meetings once a year in every area. These are more like retreats for pastors and their wives to stay together, pray together, discuss current issues, and develop deeper relationships with leaders in their area. We also have an annual conference that is more like the whole family coming together. This year we're going to have one on the East Coast and one on the West Coast. Every third year we have a combined conference in Portland, Oregon.

We also have an 800 number for our members to call free of charge. In fact, through this 800 number we can connect members to any other member in the nation. So, pastors have free access to each other. I also send periodic letters of encouragement, apostolic concerns and other things that might be of interest.

With organization, we have a skeleton. Then we have to put the flesh on it, and get life into it. But without an organization, we would go nowhere. Without a skeleton we'd just be like a jellyfish. But what makes it work is putting the flesh on it. And the flesh, the life of the fellowship, is the relationships, the interaction, the caring and loving. It is just helping each other, ministers helping ministers.

LARRY: Is your annual conference your main event? How do you strategize for that event?

DICK: Yes, it is. The Apostolic Leadership Team meets first to decide what the themes and subjects should be for the conference, including the workshops. Then Frank and I discuss with the Administrative Team who would best cover these themes. Most of our speakers are from within the fellowship with an occasional outside speaker.

LARRY: Why are you expanding to an East and West Coast annual conference?

DICK: It is very costly for all our members to fly into Portland, even though we pay the motel bill for the senior pastor members. The cost of travel can be very expensive. More and more pastors were simply not able to come to the annual conference. So we began conducting one for each coast. Again, with our priority being relationship, unless we see each other we cannot continue to grow in this way. So we do what we must to make it easier for everyone to attend.

LARRY: Are the International Fellowships having their own annual conferences?

DICK: Yes. In Europe, we have an annual conference and regional conferences as well. We have an annual conference for West Africa in Ghana, as well as a conference in Hong Kong for the Asian countries. In addition, all of our affiliate organizations have their own conferences (including Brazil, Mexico, Uganda, and Australia). Our goal is to be a catalyst to bring pastors and leaders together, to help break down the walls between people in various nations, and to try to assist them in fulfilling their destiny.

LARRY: I noticed that some apostolic fellowships or denominations have a centralized Bible college or ministry training program. Have you ever thought of having an MFI training program?

DICK: No, we believe the local church is the best ministry and leadership training ground. To start a school independently of a local church goes against our philosophy. We encourage churches all over the world to start their own training programs to develop leadership. Certainly, places like Portland Bible College, which I started in 1967, and schools like this can be a great resource to them to train teachers and draw material support, but leadership training is the function of the local church where the training can be coupled with pastoral care and ministry experience. My whole passion is to build the local church. So, as a fellowship, we would never start any kind of school.

LARRY: How many churches or pastors are involved with MFI now?

DICK: There are over 400 minister members represented in the USA. There are many more overseas when you figure the affiliated organizations. The international aspect of MFI is growing very fast right now.

Around 50 ministers in Puerto Rico just came into relationship with us. We have been invited to relate to pastors and churches in Costa Rica and Colombia, around 200 in Bogota alone. It is just kind of exploding, that's scary. I'm not looking for it, either.

I just want to make sure our fellowship here in the USA is functioning well, like a pilot program. And if it works well here, then we can export it.

Eventually, we will have indigenous fellowships in many other nations. But we want to start slow and have the right leadership team. I don't know what God's doing. Sometimes I get overwhelmed. I've never been down this road before.

It's funny, Larry, all my life I have felt like somebody has been pushing me. Personally, I'd just as soon stay right here and have my family, my fireplace, my backyard, and my Bar-B-cue, and work on my boat (which I sold for lack of attention) and my car. But there are these big hands shoving me. I hear the Lord saying, "Come on, Dick, you've got plenty time to rest in eternity." So, I just keep going, trying to keep up with the Lord in this great adventure. And I thank the Lord that he has given both my wife and I health and strength to do what He has called us to do.

LARRY: Let me ask you one more question. It seems as though quite a few apostolic networks or "tribes" are popping up these days. Have you ever given thought to having a relationship with these other apostolic networks? Will we see a growing apostolic "internet" form in the future?

DICK: We already have a relational connection with what's called the Network of Christian Ministries. That includes about sixty "tribes." We go to listen and cross-pollinate. Another apostolic network is the United Christian Fellowship led by Paul Paino. There are about a dozen fellowships our size involved. Peter Wagner has networked with several apostolic families. To partner with an apostolic family we need to share similar convictions and distinctives. I love to sit down and talk and share with others, but to make a formal agreement to relate—I'm not real comfortable with that unless it seems appropriate to everyone involved. Honestly, in many cases, we do not share the same underlying concepts. How can two walk together except they be agreed? We can be friends with anyone, but we have to be true to our own distinctives.

However, this kind of issue would be the decision of the Apostolic Leadership Team, most likely on a case by case basis.

LARRY: I suppose the Holy Spirit would just have to bring you into another apostolic leader's life and knit your heart together, so that you have a real relationship with him. Is it more of a relational thing than it is an organizational thing?

DICK: Absolutely! Whatever we do must be based on real relationship and the clear leading of the Holy Spirit. This does not mean that we are not excited about what God is doing in other groups. They all have validity. We simply must be true to who we are. We are not prepared to adjust our convictions for the sake of a structural unity. However, I want to make it perfectly clear that we want to endeavor to keep the unity of the Spirit in the bond of peace (see Ephesians 4:3), knowing that God will eventually bring us, in His time and in His way, to a unity of faith and purpose (see Ephesians 4:13).

15

THE
APOSTLE'S
ROLE TODAY

"Then Moses said to him, 'Are you zealous for my sake? Oh, that all the Lord's people were prophets and that the Lord would put His Spirit upon them!'"

(NUMBERS 11:29)

We are living in an exciting time when God is restoring His church to the original pattern given in the book of Acts. In the last fifty years, we have seen a renewed understanding of many important biblical truths that were apparently lost to the experience of the church in general. These include principles of Davidic Worship, Eldership Government, the gifts of the Spirit, and the five-fold ministry of Apostles, Prophets, Evangelists, Pastors, and Teachers.

God is trying to build the leadership of the church so that the church can truly become all that it is to become before the return of Christ. It seems that the early focus of the 60's and 70's was on the teaching ministry. In the 80's and early 90's there was a strong emphasis on the prophetic ministry. Now it appears that we are seeing a divinely inspired emphasis on the apostolic ministry.

When God restores an area of understanding to the church, He often begins as Jesus did when he came to the earth. He begins in a way consistent with the calling of Jeremiah, where He comes *"to root out and to pull down, to destroy and to throw down..."* (Jeremiah 1:10).

The Spirit of Jeremiah

When Jesus began His ministry, He came in the spirit of Jeremiah. He called the nation to repent and he challenged their traditions and ways of viewing things that were in essence making the Word of God ineffective.

He wanted to "root up" every plant that had not been planted by the Father. He came to "pull down" strongholds in their ways of thinking that were hindering them from receiving God's plan and pattern. He came to "destroy" the works of darkness that were in opposition to the truth. He came to "throw down" every lofty thought that stood against the knowledge of God. He came to challenge their historic interpretations that limited God and kept the purposes of God at bay.

The reason Jesus did this was so that He could build and plant. Jesus had a vision for a victorious church that would overcome all of the forces of darkness and establish the authority of the kingdom of God in the earth. Jesus came as the Apostle from heaven to lay the foundation for that church. Such a church would be God's instrument to establish His purpose.

God's Method of Restoration

Jesus often comes to us in the same way today. Through the history of the church, man has created His own definitions that have at times actually hindered the expression of the true. God's desire is to get us back to the truth because that is where the power can be found.

Therefore, when Jesus brings new understanding to the church in any area, He usually begins by challenging our past thought patterns and assists us, by the Holy Spirit, to reevaluate what we believe based on a fresh illumination of the Word of God.

If God's purpose is going to be accomplished prior to the second coming of Christ (and I believe it is), then the church must rise to a state that is as God intended. That means that every ministry God gave for the purpose of equipping the saints and building up the church will also have to be functioning just as God intended.

Pastors and teachers must be released, or "unmuzzled," to function according to God's design. True prophetic ministry must come forth with great power and anointing. Evangelists must help prepare the church for the great harvest at the end of the age. And apostolic ministry must take its rightful place in the midst of all of the other ministries. All are necessary if the church is to be complete.

I am thrilled to see a new emphasis on apostolic ministry. I know we are in God's prophetic timing to see a restoration of this ministry to its original splendor to the body of Christ. I know it is a key to the evangelization of the world. I know it is a key to the equipping and releasing of many laborers into the harvest.

As with all seasons of restoration, there will be a mixture at first. There will be a blending of opinions, mixed with experience, past knowledge, and limited understanding. However, if we remain patient through the process, we will see the rebirthing of a ministry that is vital to the success of the church.

A Common Ministry

The apostolic ministry in New Testament times was not a ministry that was reserved for just a few. In fact, if you simply note the occurrence of references to the various ministries mentioned in Ephesians 4, you will find that the ministry of the apostle seems to be the most prevalent. In other words, there were many apostles of all descriptions.

The Need Today

This is what is needed today. We need a redefinition of the ministry so that we can see a greater release of this ministry. We need more apostolic fathers in the body of Christ who will take responsibility for mentoring future generations of leaders. We need more apostolic church planters who will start churches in every corner of the world. We need more apostolic resources to help pastors and churches to fulfill vision and accomplish purpose.

Not every apostolic ministry will look the same. Not every apostolic ministry will have the same sphere of ministry. Not every apostolic ministry will have the same recognition and influence. Not every apostolic ministry will even recognize that they are indeed apostolic ministries. That does not matter.

What matters most is that those who feel a call to this ministry wait on God, open their hearts to His voice and leading, and become a person who is willing to lay his or her life down for others.

It Starts With the Heart

Apostolic ministry begins in the heart. It is a heart that is grateful to God for His abundant mercy. It is a heart that is broken for the lost. It is a heart that is gripped with the purpose of God. It is a heart that aches for the weak condition of the church. It is heart that yearns to see all men saved and fulfill their eternal destiny. It is a heart that is enlarged and thus has room for others.

It Grows Over Time

Apostolic ministry grows over a period of time. Many eventual apostolic ministries will grow up through one of the other ministries. God uses their involvement to expand them, give them wisdom that comes from experience, and to position them for further release and influence.

My prayer is that many who read this book would be challenged to become apostolic in heart and function. Not seeking after a title, but desiring a "good work." Not seeking to be served but to serve. Not wanting to be a lord, but to be a fathering servant. The need is great. The church is waiting. God is for you!

NOTES

1   Gerhart Kittel, *Theological Dictionary of the New Testament*,
    Vol. 1, (Grand Rapids: Eerdmans, 1964), 398-446.

2   Kevin Conner, *The Book of Acts* (Portland, Oregon: City
    Bible Publishing, 1973), 1-2.

3   French Arlington, *The Acts of the Apostles* (Peabody,
    Massachusetts: Hendrickson Publishers, 1988),
    xxxvi-xxxvii.

4   Frank J. Goodwin, *A Harmony of the Life of St. Paul* (Grand
    Rapids: Baker, 1960), np.

5   McClintock & Strong, *Cyclopedia of Biblical, Theological and
    Ecclesiastical Literature*, Vol. 1, pg. 268

6   Ibid., pg. 269